TANTRA
Hedonism in Indian Culture

Tantra in Contemporary Researches

1. Impact of Tantra on Religion and Art; by T.N. Mishra (ISBN 81-246-0073-2)
2. Lalitā-Sahasranāma — A Comprehensive Study of One Thousand Names of Lalitā Mahā-tripurasundarī; by M.L. Joshi (ISBN 81-246-0104-6)
3. Yoga-Tantra and Sensuousness in Art; by T.N. Mishra (ISBN 81-246-0239-5)
4. Tāntric Hedonism of Mahānadī Valley (Uḍḍiyāna Pīṭha); by Jitamitra Prasad Singh Deo (ISBN 81-246-0269-7)

TANTRA
Hedonism in Indian Culture

Prem Saran

D.K.Printworld (P) Ltd.
New Delhi

Cataloging in Publication Data — DK
[Courtesy: D.K. Agencies (P) Ltd. <docinfo@dkagencies.com>]

Saran, Prem, 1952-
Tantra: hedonism in Indian culture.
Includes bibliographical references (p.).
Includes Index.
ISBN 812460097X

1. Tantrism. 2. Hedonism — Religious aspects — Hinduism. I. Title.

ISBN 81-246-0097-X
First Published in India in 1994
Second impression in 1998
Third impression in 1999
Fourth impression in 2006

Published and printed by:
D.K. Printworld (P) Ltd.
Regd. office : *'Sri Kunj'*, F-52, Bali Nagar
New Delhi - 110 015
Phones : (011) 2545-3975; 2546-6019; *Fax* : (011) 2546-5926
E-mail: dkprintworld@vsnl.net
Web: www.dkprintworld.com

Cover Photo: Tantric ***yab-yum*** icon in the possession of the author.

To

My *Iccha-guru* and mentor,
the late Swami Agehananda Bharati

Foreword

In the West, pleasure or bliss, like dessert, should be taken last, after the substance of the main meal, and then in small quantities. Too much dessert, like too much pleasure, is deemed bad for a person. The health and the spirit can be weakened by these things. Pleasure, especially too much of it, is to be feared and avoided, lest a person give in to it and so succumb to moral corruption and physical decay. It is through austerity that a person achieves worthwhile ends, not through pleasure. Ecstasy is taken as evidence of madness. In India, sweets are often eaten before the meal, and in Tantric thinking and practice, pleasure or bliss is affirmed, not repressed. It is the acknowledged central force of being. Ecstasy is desired, the mystical goal. Tantric traditions, therefore, affirm the pleasurable as natural, particularly hedonistic sexual pleasure, which is an expression of *shakti*, the universal force of creation, and they use its power to achieve ecstasy or bliss.

Small wonder, then, that tantrism has inspired discomfort, if not outright fear, misunderstanding, and avoidance in those who have seen it as the antithesis of what they believe desirable. And so, too, readers should not be surprised that few scholars trained in Western traditions have had much to say about tantrism that is positive or insightful. They are made too uncomfortable by it. Until recently, scholars have instead found greater affinity with orthodox *Vedic* Hinduism, which advocates a more comfortable, familiar asceticism, as the mechanism for achieving salvation. It is this *Vedic* asceticism, Mr. Saran argues, influenced by British Victorianism, that has been the dominant source of orthodoxy in elite Indian urban society in recent centuries. But this orthodoxy has done little to limit the pervasiveness of tantric ideas in popular Indian folk culture nor to enlighten those interested in tantric perceptions. Yet these perceptions lie at the core of Hindu thinking about being and clearly have a central place in notions of the female principle, shakti, and worship of female deities. They also lie at the core of orthodox understandings of God, viz. the Hindu Tantrics' dictum: "*Shivah shaktivihinah shavah*", "Shiva without shakti is a corpse" (p. 34).

In this short book, Prem Saran, himself a tantric initiate, offers a concise and sympathetic introduction to tantrism, its place in Bengali and Assamese culture, and to a lesser extent, its place as a pervasive non-*Vedic* system of thought and ritual in Hinduism. But what the book is really and ambitiously about is a cultural critique of modern Indian values and life-ways. The reader should not look here to learn about specific tantric practices or beliefs. As cultural critique, the book is sure to offend many because Mr. Saran takes on cultural heroes such as Vivekananda and M.K. Gandhi; he also is critical of Gandhi's advocacy of the *Bhagavad Gita*, which he sees as a by-product of Gandhi's acceptance of a Victorian valuation of work as worship.

By contrast, Mr. Saran argues that tantra is juxtaposed to *Vedic* traditions as a heterodox life-affirming tradition that is both ancient and basic to Hindu interpretations of being. What makes tantra heterodox, rather than a more orthodox *yogic* system, is its use of the *Panchamakara* or five practices, most particularly, the fifth *makara*, *maithuna* or sexual intercourse, especially the literal left-hand (*vamachara*) ritual practice of *maithuna*. It is in this ritual context that women are transformed into manifestations of the goddess and men partake of shakti.

In his description of tantra, Mr. Saran associates tantric traditions with values and practices that affirm a more open "natural" society—one which he advocates—than the society he describes as dominant today. This dominant society is more authoritarian, patriarchical, and puritanical in nature, fearful of enjoyment. By contrast, in Bengal, Assam, Orissa, and Kerala this dominant culture is muted by less patriarchical customs and by stronger traditions of goddess worship. Here, in these states, there exists an alternative society; one that is free and more openly tantric in character than occurs in *Vedic* custom. Caste distinctions are somewhat muted, especially in ritual contexts. The status of women is somewhat more egalitarian than in the dominant society (e.g., women can be *gurus* in tantric custom), although women are still treated as inferiors outside the ritual setting. Individual autonomy, which is a natural by-product of the mystical experience, is the norm. Enjoyment is embraced, and humor and playfulness are affirmed. The source of this openness is that the individual uses rather than represses his powerful feelings of sexuality to achieve the mystical experience. Consequently, tantra is life-affirming.

What, then, happened to tantra that drove it from center-stage in Hindu culture? In Mr. Saran's view, the primary cause was the influence of Victorian puritanical values that were the baggage of British colonialism, English education, and the Christian missionary movement.

This is a book that is sure to make the reader think about meaning, the nature of being, and society. Mr. Saran is among those rare persons who is willing to argue that this concern is critical to the society in which he lives. In this, he is in the *parampara* of Rammohan Roy, and, as an IAS officer himself, Mr. Saran carries on the intellectual tradition of that great service.

MATTISON MINES
Professor and Chair
Department of Anthropology

University of California
Santa Barbara, California
U.S.A.

Preface

THIS book is a cultural-anthropological study of some aspects of the phenomenon of Tantrism, which has been a systematic, esoteric and hedonistic element in Indian culture from the very early Middle Ages. Tantrism is a genuine and important ***parampara***, with widespread and well-articulated ramifications throughout the social and cultural life of the pan-Indian civilization. The diffidence with which scholars generally had hitherto approached the subject has of late been replaced by an increasing confidence in its cultural importance, as is evident from the formation, a few years ago, of the "Society for Tantric Studies", an international body of scholars interested in the field, of which the author himself has been a member since its inception.

This work is *also* an essay in method, an exercise in methodology in which I have tried to apply certain anthropological tools and concepts like "Cultural Debate", "Cultural Criticism", "Hindu Renaissance" and "Pizza-effect". Of these, the last three were developed by the late Prof. Agehananda Bharati, with whom I had been in frequent correspondence during the past decade.

The various chapters are based on my articles, published and unpublished, and on my M.A. Paper written at the University of Pennsylvania. The book is basically about the Assam-Bengal region, because it was probably from here that Tantrism was exported to the rest of South Asia, and farther afield.

It is hoped that this book will help to fill an existing lacuna in the anthropology of South Asia, considering that the *hedonistic* aspects of South Asian culture have been somewhat neglected. This has partly been due to the suppression of these elements under British colonialism, and to the related hold of obsolete Victorian moral values over the minds of modern South Asians. Also, the Tantric route uses *erotic* ecstasy to fuel the drive to the goal of mystical consummation, and thus is a minority path hedged around with secrecy.

This minor opus would not have been possible without help from many. I acknowledge my debt of gratitude to the late Swami Agehananda Bharati, to whom I have dedicated this book, for his kindly interest in my scholarly aspirations; my ***diksha-guru*** Shri Kulada Sarma, for initiating me into the Tantric cult and ***sadhana***; Prof. Mattison Mines, the Chairman of the Department of Anthropology at the University of California, Santa Barbara, U.S.A., for kindly consenting to write the Foreword to the book; Dr R. D. Choudhury, Director of the Assam State Museum, Guwahati, who first suggested that I write this book; Dr Arjun Appadurai, who was my Graduate Adviser during my M.A. at the University of Pennsylvania; my close friend Ashok Sahu, IPS, for his contagiously positive outlook on life and his faith in the worth of my scholastic efforts; Shri Upen Gogoi of Guwahati, for his warm-hearted help with the manuscript and other manifold encouragement; Professors Guy Welbon of the University of Pennsylvania, A. C. Bhagawati of Guwahati University, and B. N. Saraswati of the Indira Gandhi National Centre for the Arts, as also Shri B. P. Singh, Jawaharlal Nehru Fellow and senior IAS colleague, for their warm encouragement and help; Shri N. Buragohain for preparing the manuscript on DTP; Shri Moloy Bhattacharya for help with the cover design; and the publishers, for the fine finished product.

Last but not least I owe a special debt of gratitude to my wife Geeta and five-year-old daughter Tanya, as also my parents and sisters, my father-in-law, and my uncle Dr M. N. V. Nair, for familial support and encouragement.

I may only add finally that Indian words have been put in darker italics; and they have been spelt out for the readers' convenience, for example, Krishna and Vishnu, and not Krsna and Visnu.

PREM SARAN

Contents

List of Plates

Fig. 1. Shiva and Devi represent the polar opposites, like male and female, whose union the Tantric adept experiences within himself (or herself) as the bliss *(ananda)* of yogic *samadhi* (Panchmukhi Shiva with Devi, Mandi, *c*. 1750 A.D., *Courtesy:* National Museum, New Delhi).

Fig. 2. *Kundalini-yoga* involves the visualization of *chakras*, or nodal points in the imagined yogic body; the Goddess Kundalini, imagined as a coiled serpent at the base of this body, is raised by meditation through these *chakras*, to unite with Shiva in the cranium, resulting in the bliss *(ananda)* of *samadhi* (*Courtesy:* National Museum, New Delhi).

Fig. 3. Tantrism has a positive attitude to all of life, and especially to sensuous experience, as exemplified by the explicitly detailed erotic sculpture found in all parts of India (Khajuraho: Kandariya Mahadeva Temple, south panel, *Courtesy*: Archaeological Survey of India, New Delhi).

Fig. 4. The central dictum of the Tantrics is "*Shakti vihinah Shivah shavah*"; i.e. "Shiva without Shakti is a corpse", thus implying the overwhelmingly gynocentric orientation of the cult (Dakshina Kali, and Shiva as *Shava*, Kangra, Pahari, *c*. 1800 A.D, *Courtesy*: National Museum, New Delhi).

Fig. 5. The amours of Radha and Krishna, as delightfully described in the *Gita Govinda* and other texts, have

Fig. 1. Panchmukhi Shiva with Devi, Mandi, *c*. 1750 A.D.

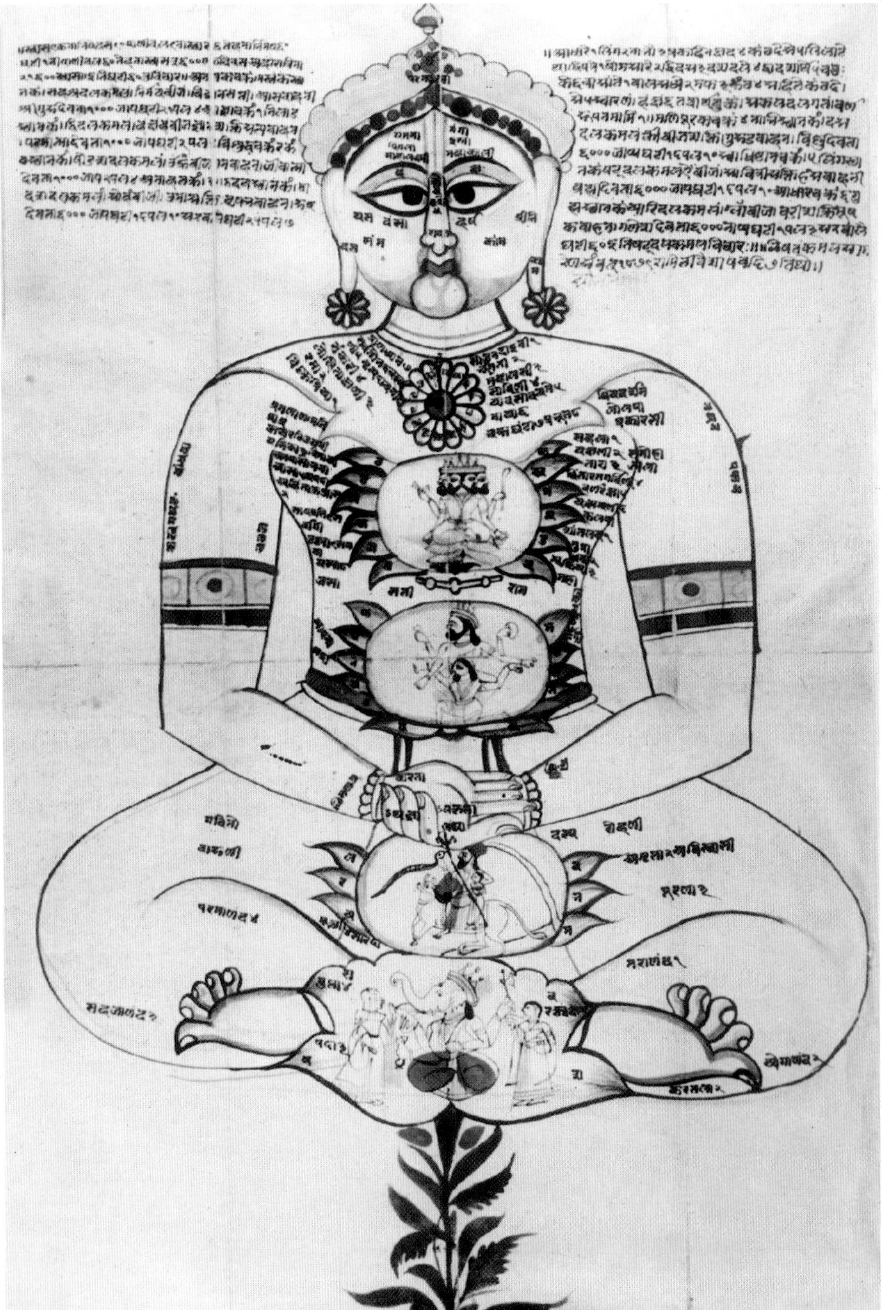

Fig. 2. Kundalini-Yoga.

Fig. 3. Khajuraho: Kandariya Mahadeva Temple, south panel.

Fig. 4. Dakshina Kali, and Shiva as *Shava*, Kangra, Pahari *c*. 1800 A.D.

Fig. 5. Radha and Krishna in Love Pavilion, Guler, *c*. 1750-1775 A.D.

Fig. 6. Khajuraho: Bharatji Temple, an amorous couple.

Fig. 7. Kahjuraho: Viswanath Temple, North Central Top panels.

Fig. 8. Gods paying homage to Devi, Kangra, Pahari, *c*. 1800-1825 A.D.

1

The Pan-Indian Tantric Tradition

LET us begin by taking a look at the historical development of Tantrism in India.

Tantrism is an important "offshoot of Hindu religiosity".[1] Till the recent past, however, it was disparaged by many Western scholars as a mixture of "magic, superstition and revolting rituals",[2] and Hindu intellectuals tend to echo these attitudes.

It was Sir John Woodroffe, a former Justice of the British High Court of Calcutta, who prepared some editions and translations of Tantric works in his *Tantrik Texts Series*, at the beginning of this century. In spite of his commendable efforts, however, Tantric studies are still inchoate, mainly because of their delicate *erotic* core.

Meaning and Scope of "Tantrism"[3]

The term "Tantra" refers to texts which expound non-***Vedic*** doctrines, especially of the ***Shakta*** variety. This tradition has been one of the *major* currents in Indian religion for the last 1,500 years, and in view of its complex nature, no single definition of the phenomenon of Tantrism is possible.

In its wider sense, Tantrism stands for practices of a *ritualistic*, sometimes magical character (e.g. ***mantra, yantra, chakra, mudra, nyasa***, etc.) These are used as a means to reach the goal of either spiritual emancipation (i.e. ***mukti***), or of more mundane aims (mainly magical domination), in various Hindu and Buddhist sects.

In a more *restricted* sense, however, Tantrism denotes a system of rituals, which are full of symbolism and are chiefly ***Shakta***, and which are propagated along "schools" (***sampradaya***) and lines of succession (***parampara***) by spiritual adepts or gurus. It is ***sadhana***, which utilizes ***Kundaliniyoga*** and other psychosomatic experiences. It is in this restricted sense that Tantrism is known, in India itself, though it is difficult to distinguish between the two meanings.

Despite this difficulty of defining Tantrism, there is indeed a salient indicator which sets it apart from Hinduism in general, and that is the Tantric ***panchamakara*** ritual, especially the *fifth* "m". Even though it is not always present, the use of the "five elements" (***panchatattva***), viz. alcohol, meat, fish, ***mudra*** (usually parched grains), and sexual intercourse (***maithuna***), is typical in Tantric worship.[4] It has been argued that the fifth element, viz. ritual sexual union with a woman previously initiated and "transformed" into the manifestation of the goddess,[5] is the *central* Tantric ***sadhana***, and that it is not really relevant whether it is literally performed (i.e. ***vamachara*** or left-handed practice) or only mentally (i.e. ***dakshinachara*** or right-handed praxis[6]). It is the actual or alleged performance of these rites which has given Tantrism its bad name in the public mind.[7]

Early History of Tantrism[8]

The Hindu religious tradition can be reduced to two chief denominators : the ***Vedic*** and the Tantric; the relations between the two are very complex. Thus, Tantrism in its *wider* sense is found in Shaivism and Vaishnavism also (and even in *Jainism*). In fact, as Chintaharan Chakravarty put it, "Brahmanic worship is all through permeated by Tantricism".[9]

Even though Tantrism is quite obviously not a mere continuation of the ***Vedic*** tradition, the points of agreement are rather striking. A number of later practices and doctrines are indeed foreshadowed by what is in some earlier *Upanishads* and even *Brahmanas*, e.g. the interiorization of sacrifice, the sexual significance of the ritual, etc. In fact, as Padoux puts it, both Hindu and Buddhist Tantrism can be described as "reinterpretations, in a new spirit, of their respective traditions".[10]

Along with its ***Vedic*** source, Tantrism is *also* rooted in very old traditions of ***yoga*** and body cult, shamanism, religious eroticism and folk ritual, dating possibly to the Indus Valley culture. The actual emergence of ***Shakta*** elements in literary sources would seem to reflect the process of absorption of local female deities with the "great tradition" Hinduism of the ***Brahmans***.

At any rate, from the fifth century onwards Tantrism becomes a pan-Indian "fashion. One meets it everywhere, in innumerable different forms".[11] It was possibly around the sixth or seventh century A.D. that Shaktism became a major factor in Indian religious life. From the Sanskrit writer Bana (seventh century A.D.) onwards, there are many references to the ***Shakti*** cult, especially to its striking aspects like human sacrifice. As for the Buddhist ***Vajrayana***, around the seventh or eighth centuries A.D., ***Siddhas*** (i.e. adepts) were associated with the royal courts of Assam, Bengal and Kashmir; this is, of course, an important indicator of the *salience* of the Tantric movement. And, in parts of Western India, the evidently Tantric ***Kapalika*** cult also became popular during this period, viz. during the seventh century A.D.

It is still a moot point as to which developed earlier, Hindu Tantrism or Buddhist Tantrism. It is perhaps more accurate to say that both were based on *older traditions* (like the body culture of the ***Siddhas***), which were handed down and developed by people who did not sometimes care very much about their doctrinal purity, though Padoux for one feels that Tantrism is basically a Hindu phenomenon. For although it is found in all Indian religions, to some extent, it has perhaps developed mainly from within the "ancient orthodox tradition".[12]

At this point, one must mention the "***Kula*** path", which developed between the fourth and ninth centuries A.D. Padoux[13] rightly points out that the Tantras use these classificatory terms (***"vama", "dakshina", "Kaula",*** etc.) very loosely, but this "***kula*** path" was nevertheless definitely the most important, certainly the most *characteristic* movement in Tantrism. And it refers essentially to the left-handed practice.[14]

Later History of Tantrism[15]

Tantrism possibly peaked around 1000 A.D. and from that time on is richly documented in written and non-written sources. Thus, there was a great popularity of erotic sculpture in this period, though these cannot automatically be attributed to Tantric influences.

Among the important Tantrically oriented teachers were Abhinavagupta and others of the Trika school of Kashmir *Shaivism*. Then, according to ***Shakta*** tradition, the famous philosopher Shankara was also very influential in promoting Tantrism. He quite possibly wrote the ***"Saundarya-lahari"***, the hymn to the goddess which established the ***Shrividya mantra*** of the "***Dakshina-charins***".[16] At any rate, according to Monier-Williams, he established a ***Shri-chakra*** (the famous Tantric ***yantra***) in each of the four monastic centres he founded. Payne, therefore, concludes that the very fact that the ***Shaktas*** could claim him as one of their own is an indication of the strength of their sect.[17]

Thus, the period from the eighth or ninth century to the fourteenth century was a "time of flourishing Tantric tradition, both textual and artistic . . . . Tantric Hinduism was then in full bloom".[18]

Then, in the fifteenth century, in the Gangetic area and in the North-East, ***Shakta*** Tantrism had to fight against *rival* movements like the ***Vaishnava*** revival. Despite this competition, however, Tantrism has persisted right down to modern times.

Social Position of Tantrics[19]

Tantrics were from all social strata. According to most Tantric texts, the rites are open to all castes and creeds all men are Shiva and all women are Shakti during the actual rites. Sometimes the texts prefer things and actions which involve the breaking of social taboos, and this was an important reason for making Tantrism disreputable with the orthodox. However, anti-caste sentiments should not be extrapolated beyond the ritual situation. It is quite possible that breaking taboos in the ritual situation was just another way to help the higher-caste Tantric get beyond his *normal* existential situation.

Another important feature of Tantrism is the position of women. Shaktism proclaims woman to be the manifestation of the Great Goddess. There are many references to female ***sadhikas***, and even ***gurus***. The fact, however, is that the chief role of women in the ***Shakta*** Tantric cult is only to be the ritual partners of the male adepts during their ***sadhana***. The important role of women in Tantrism is thus relevant only in the *ritual* setting. Here again, the "liberating antinomianism"[20] of Tantrism is in fact predicated upon the social inferiority of women.

It has often been argued that Tantrism originated in groups which belonged to the low castes, or were on the fringes of the Hinduized area. The worship of ***Devi's*** bodily parts as conducted in Kamakhya and other places may be one example of such local and agrarian cults. Thus, Bengal and Assam have been considered by some authors to be the origin of ***Shakta*** and Tantric practices.

To sum up, the Tantras did not concentrate on developing any new concepts; they often repeat truths common to Hinduism.[21] The real difference between the Tantric and non-Tantric traditions is practical : the former provides a "short-cut to redemption";[22] it is a "leap philosophy", to use Karl Potter's terminology. Thus, Tantric ritualism is closely modelled on the normative Hindu rituals; Tantrism only juxtaposes its *own* variations to the normative ones. For example, Tantrics have adopted many ***Vedic mantras***, often with very slight modifications.[23] In short, the pan-Indian Tantric tradition can be characterized as "the psycho-experimental interpretation of non-Tantric lore".[24]

References

1. Gupta et al, Preface
2. *Ibid*, p. 3
3. Gupta et al, pp. 5-9
4. Padoux, p. 279
5. *Ibid*
6. Bharati (1965 : 228-236)
7. *Ibid*
8. Gupta et al, pp. 15-25

9. *Ibid*, p. 6
10. Padoux, p. 273
11. Mircea Eliade, quoted in Padoux, p. 273
12. Padoux, p. 274
13. *Ibid*, p. 276
14. Gupta et al, pp. 40-46
15. *Ibid*, pp. 25-28
16. Bharati (1965 : 20)
17. Payne, p. 44
18. Padoux, p. 274
19. Gupta et al, pp. 29-35
20. *Ibid*, p. 34
21. *Ibid*, pp. 47-67
22. Bharati (1965 : 31)
23. Gupta et al, p. 123
24. Bharati (1965 : 20)

2

Tantrism and the Khajuraho Temples

THE Kandariya Mahadeo and other temples at Khajuraho in Madhya Pradesh are rightly famous for their exquistely crafted erotic sculptures. They belong to a class of architecture that includes, among other examples, the well-known Konarak temple in Orissa. The question that arises is why such explicit ***maithuna*** themes were depicted on *religious* edifices. Could they possibly be the expression of Tantric ideology?[1]

An authority on the Tantric cult, Agehananda Bharati has without qualification called these temples "Tantric".[2] Other scholars, Indian and Western, have not, however, been so definite; some have, in fact, *denied* that they could be Tantric. There are still others who have called them obscene, though there is quite patently a vast gulf between the blasé, dehumanizing efforts of *Playboy* magazine and its clones, and these tender and sublime religious sculptures.

Perhaps one reason why scholars have hesitated to call these sculptures Tantric lies in the cultural attitudes they hold. Many western scholars are quite possibly influenced by their Christian traditions: in Christianity, religion has a lot to do with morality, which is *not* the case in Hinduism.[3] Thus, persons brought up in the Judaeo-Christian tradition would possibly find it difficult to appreciate the use of amoral, *erotic* methods in religious experimentation.[4]

The question then arises why *Indians* should also share this value-system. The answer is perhaps equally obvious. The official culture of India has been deeply influenced by two centuries of catechization, conscious and unconscious, by British missionaries and administrators; and before that, there was the influence of seven centuries of rule by Muslims, whose ideology is similarly "Mediterranean".[5] Further, Indians suffer from a deep anxiety-syndrome regarding the loss of the semen virile;[6] this fear is linked, among other things, to the magical, cross-culturally documented fear of loss of soul. These two strands of asceticism were brought together in the Victorian personality of Mohandas Gandhi, who has had a tremendous effect on recent generations of Indians.[7] Gandhi's opinions have been criticized only by an intellectual like M. N. Roy, who pointed out, for example, that Gandhi even wanted to deface the Khajuraho sculptures![8] This shamefaced attitude is shared by most Indian scholars.

Let us now look at the social history of these temples. They were built under the aegis of the Chandella rulers of Bundelkhand, who were the dominant regional power in the tenth and eleventh centuries.[9] They built these magnificent temples partly to acquire religious merit, and partly to symbolize their power.[10]

It is possible that the Chandellas were of tribal origin, as Pramod Chandra points out.[11] That whole region of India has even today a large concentration of tribal groups; besides, this phenomenon of lower-ranked tribal and other social groups forming royal dynasties is not uncommon in Indian history.[12] These and similar groups did not share the ascetic world-view of the mainstream Indian societies.[13] This is so even today in the matrifocal areas of India, viz. Kerala, Orissa, Bengal and Assam.[14] In these comparatively open societies,[15] Tantrism has survived even into modern times;[16] and in medieval times, this cult had an even wider spread, extending into Kashmir and even into areas that are now in Pakistan.[17] The point is that a powerful royal dynasty, in a social milieu that was much less puritanical than that of modern India, had the wherewithal and the psychological security to depict Tantric rites sculpturally, assuming that the rulers or their ***acharyas*** were members of the cult.[18] If they *were* there was precious little that the establishment, i.e. ***Brahmans*** and others, could have done, especially if these temples were private shrines for royalty, as has been argued.

Let us come now to the specific opinions of art historians and other scholars. Pramod Chandra feels that the Khajuraho erotica were the work of ***Kaula*** and ***Kapalika*** cults.[19] (Without going into the exact nature of these cults, one may generally agree that they were Tantric.) Chandra feels that the ideology of these cults was above reproach, being aimed at ***moksha***, or "salvation". He, however, feels that these cults "degenerated" in time and became licentious. Such emotive terms, however, should give one pause: can one divine another's inner experiences (especially ineffable ones like the mystical), and then magisterially distinguish "proper" from "improper"? As Bharati rightly points out, mysticism cannot be qualified as either "proper" or "improper"; it is either "genuine" or "spurious".[20] Perhaps, as he also points out, what people resent here is the personal autonomy generated by the mystical experience, whether obtained by Tantric or other means.[21]

"Persuasive", not "Descriptive"

Going back to Chandra : he then quotes Kshemendra and other writers of the time, who caricatured,[22] perhaps unjustly, the Tantric ritualists by associating them with the ***Kapalikas***. Here it must be pointed out that, from the perspective of modern linguistic philosophy, terms like "degenerate" (as used in such critiques) are "persuasive", and not "descriptive".[23] Besides, the opinions of the above traditional writers may be *biased*,[24] or at best based on ignorance, because Tantrism was after all a secret cult. The members of the establishment resented this secrecy, which did not allow of inspection and control;[25] further, they (specially the ***Brahmans***) were suspicious of the anti-caste attitudes of Tantrics. Finally, they (i.e. the ***Brahmans***) also resented the fact that Tantric ritual, being an alternative route to ***moksha***, could dispense with their specialized priestly skills.

At this point, it would be appropriate to briefly summarize the Tantric ideology. Tantrics use ecstasy to lift themselves into the joy of mystical union,[26] which, as the *Taittiriya Upanishad*[27] puts it, is *much* greater than any sensual pleasure. To power their quest, Tantrics intensify and prolong ***maithuna*** by using ***mantra, yantra, kundalini yoga***, etc.[28] Thus, as Bharati explains, the ithyphallic ***yogi*** is a sublime image of *self-control*; ***maithuna*** is the replica of divine, cosmic joy, and the orgasmic moment is the nearest human approach to desirelessness.[29] As a famous Hindi poet put it, "***maithun durlabh kahan***?".[30] That is to say, even in modern puritanical India, sexual relations are not that difficult to come by. In other words, the deeper significance of Tantric ritual is rather to be seen, for example, in the late-medieval miniature paintings of royal Tantric couples in sexual union, looking *tenderly* into each other's eyes. There are quite a few similar tender postures depicted at Khajuraho.[31] This state of surrender, and of openness to intimacy and to the mystical experience, is a far cry from the rushed attitude of modern man. (It is interesting to note here that the prostitutes of nineteenth-century Calcutta called British soldiers "dunghill cocks", because of their hurried businesslike performance of the sexual act.)[32] Our modern lack of time has also interestingly been construed as a sign of puritanism by many.[33]

Returning to Khajuraho, another scholar who has written extensively on these sculptures is Devangana Desai. Sharing the puritanical world-view of modern Indians, she uses a convoluted logic to try and prove that these sculptures are *not* Tantric. She finally[34] does *concede* that they may be a symbolic depiction of the Tantric goal, but she qualifies this by primly calling them symptoms of degeneration, sexual indulgence, etc.[35] The problem faced by people like Desai is perhaps due to the Western mind-body split associated with Descartes. As Gilbert Ryle[36] has shown, the whole concept of a mind controlling the body is illusory and is caused by an improper use of language. Thus, it is not surprising that Desai and others often complain that the *mental* attitudes of all Tantrics may not be pure, and that the widespread use of such antinomian soteriological techniques would be subversive of social values.[37] The fact, however, is that Tantrics, like other

Indian mystics, have long employed ***yogic*** methods which use the body to affect the mind, since the Indian tradition does not postulate the mind-body split.[38] Further, the Indian world-view has always been in some sense asocial, since the ***sannyasi*** who *renounces* society has been the culture-hero right up to modern times.[39]

What is really resented by modern Indians perhaps is the personal autonomy generated by the mystical experience (whether obtained by Tantric or other means), whereby the mystic feels himself to be *above* societal morality.[40] This modern attitude is a far cry from that of the Indian villager, who feels that "Shiva alone can say whether a ***sannyasi*** is genuine or not",[41] and is, therefore, willing to give him the benefit of the doubt. In this connection, it has been observed that when rural people visit Khajuraho, they view these temples quite simply as part of the divine play (i.e. ***lila***).[42] They do not try to explain them away as a dubious part of the tradition, unlike modern, alienated Indians. These latter are embarrassed by a large part of their cultural heritage, especially the Tantric elements, and see it as backward and dysfunctional in the modern milieu.[43]

This value-syndrome has the strange effect of causing Devangana Desai to characterize such erotic sculpture as a *caricature* of Tantric practices![44] This is a queer argument, and would be like claiming that one would try to suppress "pornography" by *publicizing* the material in *Playboy*! Desai also tries to reduce the sculptures in question to the mere depiction of auspicious motifs, fertility cults, apotropaeic beliefs and the like.[45] This is a simplistic argument, as Vidya Prakash points out.[46]

Contradictory Arguments

Let us now take a more detailed look at some of Desai's involved and contradictory arguments. Though she does not deny the spiritual aspect of Tantrism, she feels that its goal of achieving the "Divine Bi-sexual Unity" of mysticism is not really relevant here.[47] At another point, she declares of-hand that the depiction of human sexual couples and orgies is not "functionally" (sic) related to

Tantric ***sadhana.***[48] Then, she makes another sweeping statement, viz. that magic was one of the *essential* elements of Tantrism[49]; this last is an especially meaningless characterization of a complex phenomenon like Tantrism: one may as well apply this reductionist argument to the whole of Hinduism itself ! Again, while arguing that some of the sculptures at Khajuraho are caricatures, she herself admits that she is basing her opinion on the accounts of *opponents* of Tantric and related practices ![50] Finally, she makes the specious argument that Tantra is essentially ***hatha-yoga,*** and since some of the male lovers in the sculptures have protruding stomachs, they could not be Tantrics.[51] This is rather uninformed, because ***hatha-yoga*** is the very lowest, i.e. preliminary, of the eight stages of classical ***yoga.***

All this represents a rather unsophisticated, even philistine, attitude towards these multivalent sculptures, the sole aim being to deny their *Tantric* nature. Thus, L. K. Tripathi identifies some of the protagonists as Digambara Jain monks, the purpose of depicting such erotic scenes being a way to condemn such objectionable practices.[52] Even if we allow that the self-mortifying practices of the Jains could encompass such erotic and antinomian sexual techniques, Tripathi's argument is as far-fetched as Desai's similar one about these sculptures being caricatures, which we have already rebutted above.

Viewed from another angle, however, Tripathi's claim about the Digambara Jain monks is grist for the Tantric mill. Tantrics view sexual repression as counter-productive; they suggest that instead of "killing" the senses, one should harness them and thus make *easier* progress to the goal of mystical union. Thus, by turning Tripathi's argument on its head, one could argue instead that these depictions may indeed be of Jain monks, but made by *Tantrics* to ridicule the hypocritical, self-righteous pretensions by ascetics of having controlled their senses.

Further, one rationale for creating these sculptures was the concept of ***drishti-shuddhi***[53] whereby the worshipper feasts his eyes on these and other scenes of social life and so on, before entering the dark ***garbha-griha*** with his mind thereby emptied of worldly thoughts and thus ready for communion with the divine. The position of the sculptures, their size and numbers readily lend themselves to such an interpretation, which is in line with the Tantric ideology of ritual sex being a means towards the experience of the divine.

Vedic Ontology Reflects Sexual Symbolism

Let us now sample modern Western attitudes to these erotic sculptures. In an article on the "metaphysical architecture" of the Kandariya Mahadeva temple, Robert Forman argues that these sculptures have received more attention than their numbers deserve, and that the latter-day interest in them stems more from "modern eros than from Hindu theos".[54] This type of quantitative argument is irrelevant here: one may as well argue that morality, and social life in general, are determined by the values of the silent majorities in the highly diversified Western societies.[55] Besides, in the Indian canonical tradition, a single mention is sufficient to establish authority.[56] Numbers do not enter the picture at all. As for the argument about modern prurience, this may hold only for the modern West, which may (rightly or wrongly) be characterized as obsessed with sex.[57] And this obsession may be a reaction to the Christian heritage of these societies: even today, in some parts of the USA., certain kinds of heterosexual activity between consenting adults are still felonies. In contrast, the Indians who covered their *religious* edifices, no less, with these erotic sculptures, had a more complaisant attitude to sex as being one of the valued aspects of life. Further, since the ***"Kama-shastras"*** were semi-*canonical* texts, it should not be surprising that Tantrics could use sex as a stepping-stone to the divine: for the Tantric, his ritual partner is a revelation of the *mysterium tremendum*. As Radhakamal Mukherjee points out, between the tenth and thirteenth centuries, India "universally accepted the ***yoga*** of sexual conjugation as the door to . . . full spiritual awareness . . . . This is the core of the ***Kaula marga***".[58] Finally, regarding the mystical doctrine of Divine Bi-sexual Unity, i.e. the trans-sexual *coincidentum oppositarium* or "*unio mystica*", Coomaraswamy remarks that the entire ***Vedic*** ontology is typically expressed in terms of sexual symbolism.[59]

The same attitude of *downplaying* these sculptures is exhibited by Zannas in her book, *'Khajuraho'*.[60] She feels that it would be "wrong to attach too much importance" to them.[61] She says, "They represent little more than an offical interest in the stylized eroticism which is typical of this period, as much at Khajuraho as at Bhuvanesvara, Orissa".[62] This "zeitgeist" explanation is, however, too vague and unsatisfactory. There must be more to these sculptures than the style of the times: perhaps the real explanation is that the makers of these sculptures *did* subscribe after all to the Tantric ideology, and created these sculptures to celebrate their cultic belief in the Tantric way of attaining ***moksha.***

In another book, also called *'Khajuraho'*, Vidya Prakash on the other hand rightly tries to show that these erotic sculptures were a *logical* outcome of the culture of those times.[63] Thus, the erotic scenes are depicted on the temple walls "with the same profusion of detail as any other aspect of life."[64] Further, he points out that by the ninth century, sculpture became an essential part of the temple; this included erotic sculptures, which were occasionally carved at very prominent places in the temple, as at Khajuraho and Konarak.[65] He then argues that at least some of these may be "affiliated with rites and practices of Tantric cults, predominant in this age and also in this region".[66] In the concluding paragraph of his book he finally states firmly, "Some scenes are clearly a direct representation of Tantric rituals."[67]

Perhaps Polemical, But Justified

Let us recapitulate our arguments at this point, before we consider the logic of the *positioning* of these sculptures. We have so far seen the views of some scholars, Indian and Western, who are mostly unwilling to grant that the Khajuraho sculptures may indeed be Tantric. We have also pointed out some of the reasons for this strange reluctance to call a spade a spade. Our arguments may sound polemical, but they are really quite justified as a *corrective* to the scholarly neglect of this interesting part of the Indian tradition. As Bharati put it aptly, "For this omission, there is positively no excuse, unless prudishness, fear of social and scientific opprobrium, and other items of the puritanical calculus were held to be valid excuses."[68]

Now, conceding as Vidya Prakash does that some at least of these erotic sculptures may be representations of Tantric rituals, let us conclude our argument by considering the architectural logic behind their positioning, vis-a-vis the over-all scheme of the temple structure. This has been described with insight by Meister, in his article on "punning" in temple architecture.[69] He points out that most prominent erotic scenes at Khajuraho are on the ***kapili***, or juncture wall connecting the main sanctum and the ***mandapa*** in front. The ***kapili*** walls are functionally "walls of architectural conjunction",[70] as he puts it. He uses Sanskrit etymology and grammar (viz. the word ***samgam***, the root ***kam***, and the grammatical ***samdhi*** rules) to indicate the intentional pun behind this positioning.[71]

To clinch the point, he turns to iconography and refers to conjoint images of deities which can be seen on some similar temples, e.g. of Harihara, Ardhanarisvara, and even one conjoint of Shiva and Brahma. All these conjunct images are placed on the juncture wall. He concludes, therefore, "Architects at Khajuraho have struck on the same location faced with the need to give prominent place to scenes of ritual and physical union."[72] In addition, he points out, "The temples at Khajuraho in fact show a progression in the development of this sexual imagery . . . . Thus the trinity of Brahma, Vishnu and Shiva is represented on the descending levels on the ***kapili*** wall. Only Shiva's level shows lovers in sexual conjunction."[73] Finally, Meister notes that the Lakshmana temple hints at a "subtle hierarchy of religious union."[74] This is in line with the Tantric ideology, whose redemptive goal is the mystical experience of the "Divine Bi-sexual Unity" referred to earlier, which is *trans-sexual.*

We may thus conclude that some of the famous erotic sculptures at Khajuraho are indeed quite possibly Tantric, though of course in these matters "there is no hard and fast rule which would apply without any possible modification."[75]

References

1. *Cf.* Tucci
2. Bharati (1976 a : 299)
3. Bharati (1981 : 13)
4. Bharati (1977 : 195)
5. Bharati (1978 : 319)
6. Bharati (1977 : 230)
7. *Ibid*
8. Bharati (1978 : 299)
9. Chandra, pp. 98 and 100
10. *Ibid*, p. 98
11. *Ibid*
12. *Cf.* e.g. the Nayars or "royal ***shudras***", vide Bharati (1977 : 91)
13. Bharati (1978 : 334-336)
14. *Ibid*
15. *Ibid*
16. Bharati (1977 : 42)
17. Bharati (1978 : 81)
18. Desai (1975), pp. 135 and 141
19. Chandra, p. 103, n. 1
20. Bharati (1977 : 213)
21. *Cf.* chh. 10
22. *Cf.* Chandra
23. Bharati (1977 : 51)
24. Desai (1984 : 149)
25. Bharati (1977 : 137)
26. For a definition of "mystic", *cf.* Chh. 4
27. *Ibid*, p. 29-30
28. For a definition of "Tantra", *cf.* Chhs. 1 and 10
29. Bharati (1978 : 331)
30. *Ibid*, p. 284
31. *Cf.* Plates 69, 111, etc. in Desai (1975), and Fig. 7 in Chandra
32. *Cf.* Rawson
33. Bharati (1977 : 95)
34. Desai (1975 : 153)
35. *Ibid*, p. 2
36. *Cf.* Ryle
37. Desai (1975 : 122)
38. Bharati (1977 : 125-126)
39. *Ibid*, p. 55
40. *Ibid*, pp. 199-200
41. *Ibid*, p. 170
42. Bharati (1981 : 61)

43. Bharati (1977 : 230)
44. *Cf.* Coomarswamy
45. Desai, 1981
46. Prakash, pp. 153-154
47. Desai (1975 : 5)
48. *Ibid*, p.144
49. *Ibid*, p. 145
50. Desai (1984 : 149)
51. Desai (1975 : 138)
52. *Cf.* Tripathi
53. Bharati (1978 : 331)
54. *Cf.* Forman.
55. Bharati (1977 : 202)
56. Bharati (1976a : 283)
57. *Cf.* Foucault
58. Mukherji, p. 192
59. *Cf.* Coomarswamy
60. *Cf.* Zannas, Eliky
61. *Ibid*, p. 66
62. *Ibid*, pp. 79-80
63. Prakash, Preface, p. xii
64. *Ibid*, p. 178
65. *Ibid*, p. 175
66. *Ibid*, p. 82, n. 4
67. *Ibid*, p. 187
68. Bharati (1967a : 9)
69. *Cf.* Meister. (This chapter is in fact based on a term-paper which I wrote in his course on "Hindu Temple Architecture", during my M.A. at the University of Pennsylvania)
70. *Ibid*, p. 227
71. *Ibid*
72. *Ibid*, p. 228
73. *Ibid*
74. *Ibid*
75. Bharati (1967a : 229)

3

The Tantric Tradition in Bengal

WE have seen by now that Tantrism lies at the very core of the Hindu tradition.[1] As Kees W. Bolle puts it, "the Tantric movement . . . [is of] vital importance to Hinduism as a whole and not just to some esoteric devotees . . ."[2]

Also, Tantrism has been especially popular in certain regions like Bengal. In fact, Payne goes so far as to say that the greatest hold of ***Shakta*** worship has been in the Bengal region.[3] Let us, therefore, now look at the Tantric tradition of Bengal in some detail.

Bengali Tantric Literature

Just as in the rest of the country, where the emotional appeal of the many vernacular songs on Tantric themes is still alive, in Bengal too the songs of Ramprasad on Kali are still popular today, even among non-Tantrics. The ***Kapalika*** and the cremation-ground figure prominently in these Tantric songs.[4]

Such songs and ballads have become an integral part of ritual, in its private and public forms. Thus, ballads to the Goddess are ceremonially sung during her annual festival. And at this point, it may also be noted that in parts of Bengal, Durga is first worshipped by untouchable priests and only then by ***Brahmans***, since this is supposed to please the Goddess.[5]

We may now turn to particular aspects of the Bengali Tantric literature.

(i) The Charyapadas[6]

The ***Charya*** literature of the Tantric ***Siddhas*** has been called the first significant expression of the "peculiar style and temper of the Bengali people".[7] Being mostly Buddhist, the ***Siddhas*** were very much opposed to Brahmanical orthodoxy and to the caste system. This spirit largely influenced the course of Bengali literature.

These songs are the oldest literary record of Bengali and of the other languages of the region, and date from before the tenth century A.D. They became very popular because of their simplicity, and deep religious emotion. The ***Siddhas*** who wrote them were mainly Vajrayanist ***yogins,*** but they wrote for the ordinary people. The unconventional nature of their religious practices is conveyed by symbols such as that of the ***Brahman*** who is attracted to the charming but ritually impure ***Dombi*** or washerwoman. We have also seen in the first Chapter that these ***Vajrayana Siddhas*** were also associated with the royal courts, e.g. during the Pala dynasty.

(ii) Influence of Vaishnavism

The next distinct phase in the Bengali Tantric tradition was a result of the Vaishnavite revival in the fourteenth and fifteenth centuries. The influence of ***Vaishnava*** religion and literature moulded the attitudes of late-medieval ***Shakta*** Tantrics. Thus, the concept of ***bhakti,*** which emphasizes the personalistic aspect of the divine, came to be important even for Bengali ***Shakta*** groups in this period.

By then, Tantrism had become an established tradition in the Bengal region. Great Tantrics, like Krishnananda Agamavagisha (c. 1500 A.D.), had composed important Sanskrit works on Tantric ritual and theology. Maithili poets like Vidyapati had written ballads and songs about the Goddess, which greatly influenced Bengali Tantrism. The local courts were of ***Shaiva*** or ***Shakta*** faith, and ***Shakta*** literature enjoyed royal patronage and became part of the official vernacular literature.

Then, due to the Vaishnavite influence, ***bhakti*** themes like the ***lila*** of the young Krishna inspired the Tantric poets. This was reflected in the Tantric image of the Goddess as Kumari, the virgin Uma, which inspired devotees to love her like a doting father would. The motif of the mother separated from her newly-wed daughter (as Menaka was separated from Parvati, when the latter married Shiva) was culturally very fertile. Thus, the autumnal Durga festival is a time of family reunion and joy, and the daughter's visit is like Uma herself visiting her natal home.

From the late-medieval period, Bengal produced a vast body of Tantric literature. Late-seventeenth and early-eighteenth century Bengal witnessed a revival of creative Hindu Tantrism, which produced a body of mystic hymns full of emotional devotion (i.e. ***bhakti***) to the Goddess. Many ***Shakta*** temples were established, mainly dedicated to Kali.[8]

In the eighteenth century, the lyric poems (***padas***) of the great ***Vaishnava*** poets became very influential in Bengal. Among Tantrics also, devotional songs about the Goddess replaced ballads; the songs of Ramprasad especially became very popular among the common people. He introduced a new style of ***Shakta*** poetry by combining the earlier lyric tradition of the ***Charyapadas*** with Vaishnavite ***bhakti,*** and this innovation became very popular.

The era of Ramprasad was one in which the earlier sectarian exclusiveness was replaced by a religious syncretism. Themes about the playful and popular Krishna were used to express delicate emotions, even by the worshippers of Kali. (The development of a common Bengali literary culture had actually started in the seventeenth century.) Thus, Ramprasad declared that there was really no difference between Kali and Krishna. This harmony was maintained even into the late-nineteenth century by poets like Kamalakanta Bhattacharya. The neo-***Shakta*** movement of the eighteenth century found its culmination in the figure of the great nineteenth-century mystic Ramakrishna.

(iii) Vaishnava-Sahajiyas, Bauls, etc.

There is also in Bengali a large body of Tantric literature by ***Vaishnava-Sahajiyas, Bauls*** and ***Natha-Siddha yogins.*** All three groups followed similar methods of esoteric ritual and meditation. The first group has produced a large number of treatises on their doctrines and sexual-***yogic*** practices, which are similar to early Hindu and Buddhist

Tantric literature. Their adored deity is Radha, the beloved of Krishna. These Bengali Tantras were composed between the seventeenth and nineteenth centuries. Influenced by Chaitanya's Vaishnavite movement, their fervent religious aesthetics is very different from that of the impersonal Sanskrit Tantras. Their doctrines, however, did influence some ***Shakta*** practitioners, and the poet Kamalakanta compared the rise of ***Kundalini*** to the ***sahasrara*** with Radha's secret visit to Krishna.

The Vaishnava-Sahajivya Cult

At this stage, let us take a more detailed look at this interesting cult, because it represents the interaction between ***Shakta*** Tantric and non-Tantric ideas and practices in Bengal.

The term ***sahaja*** means "easy" or "natural" and refers to the fact that the cult *uses,* and does not *suppress,* the power of the senses. The eighth or ninth-century ***Charyapadas*** are clearly ***Sahajiya*** in doctrine, and so the ***Sahajiya*** cult is clearly rooted in the ancient Tantric tradition.[9]

This centuries-old ***Sahajiya*** tradition blended with the Vaishnavite, producing that interesting hybrid the ***Vaishnava-Sahajiya*** cult. The ***Sahajiya*** tradition was humanistic and monistic, while the Vaishnavite was theistic and dualistic. Again, the former viewpoint corresponded with the erotic religious sculptures at Konarak and Khajuraho; the latter world-view was much less obviously amorous, and represented the contrary view of love in religion as exhibited in Indian culture.[10]

The ***Sahajiya*** tradition took up many features of the ***Vaishnava*** in blending with the latter, e.g. the whole Radha-Krishna complex. The ***Sahajiyas,*** however, took *literally* what the ***Vaishnavas*** meant figuratively.[11] For the former, the union of Radha and Krishna was also to be experienced *physically* by the adept, in conjunction with his female partner.[12]

On the other hand, the Vaishnavite tradition in turn was also influenced by the long-existing ***Sahajiya***/Tantric tradition, both before and during the time of Chaitanya.

For example, at least two of Chaitanya's early companions had some links with the ***Sahajiya*** tradition. The first, Nityananda, was probably a member of a lefthanded Tantric order of ***Avadhutas*** or practitioners; further, one of his wives, Jahnavi, was a ***Sahajiya*** leader herself! The other, Ramananda Raya, practised a technique of chastity with two beautiful girls, which involved treating them rather intimately (like bathing and dressing them), but without sexual intercourse. This was in fact a part of the ***Sahajiya*** discipline of serving the woman as the divine Radha.[13]

In addition, Chaitanya is recorded as having loved the erotic lyrics of Jayadeva, and of the Bengali Chandidasa and the Maithil Vidyapati. Though Jayadeva may not have been a ***Sahajiya,*** similar traditions about the other two poets have more basis. In short, there is thus every possibility that Chaitanya himself was quite influenced by the ***Sahajiya*** movement.[14]

Let us turn finally to the respective position of women among the ***Vaishnava-Sahajiyas*** and among the ***Vaishnavas.*** We have seen above that Jahnavi-Devi was a "Tantric and ***Sahajiya*** leader";[15] she succeeded her husband as the "leader of a considerable ***Sahajiya*** group".[16] It bears emphasis here that it is only in the Tantric tradition that a woman may become a ***guru.***[17]

Women were respected among the orthodox ***Vaisnavas*** as well, because of the importance of Radha in Bengal, and probably also because of the Tantric tradition. In this, the ***Vaishnavas*** had come a long way from Chaitanya's own feeling that even conversation with a woman was inimical to true ***bhakti.***[18]

To sum up, the Tantric tradition had quite a favoured position in the cultural history of Bengal, and it was able to maintain its own even against the powerful Vaishnavite revival inaugurated by Chaitanya. The Tantric and non-Tantric streams blended in the ***Vaishnava-Sahajiya*** cult. Due to the high position of Radha in Bengali Vaishnavism, as the embodiment of ***prema*** or true love for Krishna, and also probably due to Tantric influences, there was a change even in the ascetic ***Vaishnava*** attitudes towards women.[19] As Padoux puts it, "Though the spirit of Tantrism is in many ways opposed to that of ***bhakti,*** both can be reconciled and are even promiscuously associated by the ***Vaishnava Sahajiya***."[20]

References

1. Bharati (1978 : 168)
2. Bolle (1965), Foreword, p. XVI
3. Payne, p. 7
4. Gupta et al, pp. 173-201
5. Payne, p. 70
6. *Cf.* Mojumder
7. *Ibid*, Foreword by Sibnarayan Ray, p. xiii
8. Bhattacharya (1974 : 153)
9. Edward C. Dimock, Jr. (1966 : 35)
10. *Ibid*, p. 1
11. *Ibid*, p. 36
12. *Ibid*, p. 15
13. *Ibid*, pp. 43-55
14. *Ibid*, pp. 56-67
15. *Ibid*, p. 52
16. *Ibid*, p. 98
17. *Ibid*, pp. 96-98
18. *Ibid*, pp. 99-101
19. *Ibid*, p. 16
20. Padoux, p. 277

4

Chaitanya, Tantrism and Hedonism in Bengal

THE element of pleasure has not been *explicitly* brought out in writings on religion. In this chapter, therefore, I shall look at the case of the mystic Chaitanya, and the *hedonistic* element in his movement of religious revival.

It has amply been realized nowadays that for studying old civilizations like the Indian which have a rich literary tradition, synchronic anthropology has only limited utility. Anthropological studies of Indian culture should, therefore, be informed by Indological and such knowledge. So I shall first briefly outline the cultural background of Chaitanya's movement.

The world-view of Indians is religious, rather than secular. Whatever secular component is present in it is the gift of British colonialism in India, as Bharati has pointed out.[1] Further, Indian ideas of time are cyclical, unlike the Western linear view. The monk or ***sannyasi*** is the charismatic of society. The individual and his works, still less the social reality, are not important, because they are seen against a "cosmic" background. Western observers tend to call this "fatalism", but from an anthropologist's perspective, this is perhaps "persuasive", not *"descriptive"* language.[2]

Before going on to describe Chaitanya's movement, I should make explicit what I mean by "mystic". I am using Bharati's definition; he calls a mystic one who intuits his numerical oneness with the ground of being, and who uses the available *ecstatic* means to attain this state.[3]

Let us come now to our protagonist. A society as positively concerned with mysticism as the Indian has, not surprisingly, produced many mystics; the "great sixteenth-century ***Vaisnava*** revivalist Chaitanya"[4] was one such. His movement spread over a large part of eastern India, and even today this tradition is very much alive there. Even today people actively worship Krishna, who is the reincarnation of Vishnu, one of the great gods of Hindu polytheism. Krishna-worship would even seem to be catching on in the West in the form of the Krishna Consciousness cult, even though it is a spurious,[5] non-genuine mutation.

Chaitanya was "a religious leader of no ordinary power".[6] And the time was ripe for his "ideas and qualities".[7] Various things contributed to this ripeness: "the decay and subsequent 'corruption' of Buddhism, the prevalence of extreme Tantric schools with their potential licentiousness, the aridness and dogmatic rigidity of Brahmanism in both social and religious spheres, and the impact of Islam, especially Sufi Islam with its emotionalism. Not only in Bengal but all across northern India in the fourteenth and fifteenth centuries there burst forth a 'romantic' enthusiasm. . ."[8]

"Viswambhara — he took the name Krishna-Chaitanya after his initiation into an ascetic order — was born . . . in 1486 . . . in Navadvip (in Bengal) . . . Very little can be learned of (his) early childhood . . . It is claimed by his biographers that he was a brilliant scholar . . . (but) he has left us no writings except for eight short devotional verses in Sanskrit.

". . . when he was twenty-two, he made a trip to Gaya, to perform in that holy place his father's funeral rites . . . . While there he accepted as ***guru*** (teacher) Isvara Puri, an 'emotional ascetic'. He returned to Navadvip God-maddened and within a short time became the centre of frenzied devotional activity in that city. For a year he lived amid wild religious enthusiasm, with nightly singing of devotional songs and ecstatic dancing . . . . He entered an ascetic order, taking this initiation at the hands of Kesava Bharati and with it the religious name Krishna-Chaitanya . . . .

"He stayed for the rest of his life in Puri, except for

an occasional pilgrimage. Here his friends and disciples from Bengal visited him annually at the time of the Car Festival. He died in 1533 . . . The least orthodox biography, and probably the most factual one, says that he injured his foot during his frenzied dancing and died from an infection".[9]

After his death, "the revival he inspired encompassed the greater part of the populations of those areas now known as Bengal (both modern Bangladesh and West Bengal), Orissa, Assam, and Bihar . . .".[10] Even while he lived, people considered him divine. Some thought he was an ***avatara,*** an incarnation of Krishna; some thought he was Krishna himself."[11]

Three Discrete Characteristics

"This enthusiastic movement had three discrete characteristics: its expression was through the vernacular languages, not through Sanskrit; it rejected the role of the Brahmin (priest) as ritual intermediary between man and God, in some ways and times going further and rejecting caste entirely; and it propagated enthusiastic religion, with singing and dancing as a part of the search for immediate and ecstatic communion with the divine.[12] The technique for mystic communion consisted basically of devotees sitting in a circle and singing devotional songs, or ***kirtanas,*** to the accompaniment of musical instruments and dancing.

"The doctrines of the new sect were codified by six of Chaitanya's followers who were scholars and theologians, called the six Gosvamis. They produced over 219 different works in Sanskrit . . . tying every teaching of the Bengal school into the orthodox traditions of Indian religion. They created a great corpus of canonical works. . .".[13]

Chaitanya was also influenced by the all-pervasive *Tantric* tradition of Bengal. The Gosvamis themselves were greatly influenced by the Tantras, perhaps even by the more antinomian *left-handed* Tantrism of the ***Sahajiyas.*** Thus, for example, the long-existing ***Sahajiya*** tradition provided the Vaishnavites with their ecstatic, mystic theory of the dual incarnation of Chaitanya as Radha and Krishna.

Analysis

As La Barre commented in his bibliographic essay on "Crisis Cults",[14] taxonomies of revitalization movements are not very useful. That work has been done quite some time back, by Wallace and others. So I shall content myself taxonomically by pointing out that the revitalization movement described here is *"redemptive"*, to use Aberle's terminology.[15] I shall turn instead to a consideration of the *ecstatic* and other connected *hedonistic* aspects of this movement. I propose to bring out these elements by juxtaposing the Indian and the Western cultural traditions. If I sound polemical, it is because I use as my tool Bharati's concept of "cultural criticism".[16] This refers to the pointed criticism of the aesthetic or other aspects of a culture, whereby the anthropologist elicits data from informants in order to elucidate its structure, dynamics, etc.

As La Barre has pointed out, Aberle's classification of revitalization movements is inadequate. It is based on the stingy, economic concept of "relative deprivation". Again, Barbara Lex has commented that "scant attention has been addressed to the *pleasurable* emotions that are educed by participating in such movements".[17] She adds, "one need not invoke the strains produced by clashing cultures or the boredom of modern civilized life to understand the attractiveness of transcendent ecstasy, whatever means are employed to that end, by human beings in any society at any time."[18] In this connection, one may also refer to Bharati's remark that the mystical experience is a "peak experience, in one category perhaps with totally consummated erotic experiences . . .".[19]

One reason why the ecstatic element in revitalization movements has been *underplayed* could be the Judaeo-Christian orientation of most observers, who have been Western. As Bharati points out, the Judaeo-Christian tradition has tended to shortchange ecstasy.[20] Then, another reason could be that, as Bharati again remarks, academics fear ecstasy because of the "endless circumlocutions" that are part of the academic life.[21]

The same scholar has identified the need for ecstasy as the *raison d'etre* of the Krishna Consciousness and other pseudo-Eastern cults that are in vogue in the West.[22] He has brought out the nexus between mysticism, ecstasy and autonomy: most people are conformists who fear autonomy in themselves and others, and ecstasy tends to generate autonomy.[23] Further, he suggests that mystic experimentation could have great therapeutic value in the West, where many people who are at odds with society are labelled paranoid-schizophrenic and shut up in mental hospitals. This line of thinking echoes the writings of people like R.D. Laing and Thomas Szasz, who deny that there is any such thing as mental disease.[24]

In India, on the other hand, many so-called "paranoid-schizophrenic" people have been, and still are, venerated as mystics.[25] Mysticism generates charisma for the Indian,[26] because in Indian culture the numinous is intuited in every phenomenon.[27] The Indian world-view is overwhelmingly religious, and monks and mystics are the culture-heroes.[28] The impersonal *monistic* theology of ***Advaita*** has had the greatest prestige, compared to the personalistic and dualistic theisms.[29] ***Advaita*** is very like ***Mahayana*** Buddhism, which is atheistic but has a very high numinous content, unlike a theology like Calvin's which is highly theistic but has hardly any numinous content.[30]

A look at traditional Indian exegesis will further elucidate the *ecstatic* core of the mystical experience. The canonical Hindu scriptures have, more than two thousand years ago, defined the mystical experience as ***ananda,*** i.e. "bliss".[31] Also, the world is ***lila*** or "divine play". I may mention in passing here that Norbeck, in his writings on "rites of reversal", has remarked on the interesting role of play in religion.[32]

To return to my main argument: ***yoga,*** which is a technique of mystic union, has been, as Bharati said, the one distinctive Indian contribution to the world.[33] It generates an "inurement against the vicissitudes of life".[34] Further, Indian lore pays a lot of "overt positive attention to the madness of mystic language" and behaviour,[35] in other words to their autonomic and *hedonistic* aspects.

The above is of course in crass contrast to Western

traditions. For one thing, Christian mystics have had few foci for meditation other than the masochistic martyr-figure of the crucified Christ, as pointed out by the Trappist monk Thomas Merton.[36] For another, Christian mystics who reported their experiences in direct, monistic and ecstatic language were persecuted: Meister Eckhart died in a dungeon, and Bruno at the stake.[37]

I shall rest my argument here, presuming that I have successfully brought out the ecstatic, hedonistic elements in religious behaviour, as exemplified by Chaitanya's revivalist movement and its interface with the Tantric tradition of Bengal.

References

1. Bharati (1982)
2. *Cf.* Stevenson
3. Bharati (1977 : 31)
4. Dimock (1966 : 10)
5. Bharati (1978 : 84)
6. Dimock, op cit, p. 26
7. *Ibid*
8. *Ibid*
9. *Ibid*, pp. 30-31
10. *Ibid*, p. 26
11. *Ibid*, p. 32
12. *Ibid*, pp. 26-27
13. *Ibid*, p. 71
14. *Cf.* La Barre
15. *Cf.* Aberle. (This Chapter is based on a term-paper, which I wrote in Prof. Anthony F. C. Wallace's course on "Revitalization Movements", during my M.A. at the University of Pennsylvania.)
16. Bharati (1978 : 259 ff.)
17. *Cf.* Lex
18. *Ibid*
19. Bharati (1977 : 75)
20. *Ibid*, p. 233
21. *Ibid*, p. 64
22. *Ibid*, p. 233
23. *Ibid*, pp. 202-203; *cf.* also Saran (1985)
24. Bharati (1977 : 117)
25. *Ibid*, pp. 196-197
26. *Ibid*, p. 162
27. Bharati (1978 : 332)
28. *Ibid*, p. 57

29. *Ibid*, p. 110
30. *Ibid*, p. 325
31. Bharat (1977 : 29)
32. *Cf.* Bharati (1976 b)
33. Bharati (1977 : 57)
34. Bharati (1977 : 75)
35. *Ibid*, p. 196
36. *Ibid*, p. 126
37. *Ibid*, p. 195

5

"Cultural Debate" and Tantrism in Modern Bengal

IN this chapter,[1] we shall examine Bengali attitudes towards Tantrism, during the period 1857 to 1947. Since, however, Tantric studies are still in their infancy, our topic has to be approached rather indirectly. Two anthropological concepts will be used as heuristic tools for the purpose.

The *first* one is David Parkin's concept of *"cultural debate"*. He looks at culture as a system of communication, of 'live exchanges in . . . 'the long conversation between the generations'".[2] This conversation is often likely to be about the values of the socio-cultural group or of some members of it, e.g. whether these values are threatened. By definition, a lot of the conversation called culture goes on *within* the group; and the threats to its values are often seen by the people in authority to arise from "the enemy or sinner within"[3] From this angle, the threatening values are seen as conflicting with those that impose order and stand for continuity, by the people who are in authority and have vested interest in the status quo.

From another viewpoint, however, according to Parkin, "these opposed forces of *emic* order and disorder can be seen as attempts to turn the long conversation between the generations into an *open debate*, a debate that may invite participants from outside the culture".[4] (Emphasis mine).

It is this concept of "cultural debate" that provides us with a very fertile tool to study attitudes towards Tantrism.

The *second* conceptual tool is Bharati's term *"pizza-effect"*. It is related to the first, in that it represents an aspect of the external dimension of the "cultural debate" in question. According to Bharati, during the past one hundred years or so, Indians have often become interested in items of their culture, *once* these were appreciated by Western thinkers and scholars. Thus, ***yoga,*** Indian classical dance and other Indian cultural artifacts, which had been *neglected* by urban Hindus, became popular when they became well known in the West.[5] This is similar to the way in which *pizza,* which was a simple bread in nineteenth-century Italy, became embellished with many additions in America, and the new dish became very popular back home in Italy.[6]

I propose to use the above two conceptual tools in conjunction with a diachronic approach. I shall look first at the debate around Tantrism as it developed in India through the centuries, until we reach the period we are actually interested in, i.e. until 1857. This is necessary in order to appreciate the *continuities* in the debate, and thus to see how that debate changed during our period of focus.

Before we proceed further, a word about the time-frame of the topic would be in order. The year *1857* was the year of the Indian mutiny, which led the very next year to the direct rule over the East India Company's Indian territories by the British Crown, and to all the influences which that rule set in motion. The year *1947* is the year of Indian independence from British rule.

The next thing to do is to recapitulate what we mean by Tantrism. We have already seen that Tantrism denotes a system of rituals, which are full of symbolism and are chiefly ***Shakta,*** and which are propagated along "schools" (***sampradaya***) and lines of succession (***parampara***) by spiritual adepts or ***gurus.*** Also it is ***sadhana,*** which utilizes ***kundalini-yoga*** and other psychosomatic experiences.

The Tantric ***sadhana*** is a purely *individual* path to release, accessible to all people, women as well as men (at least in theory), householders as well as ascetics.[7] Its *doctrinal* aspect is summed up by Madeleine Biardeau as "an attempt to place '***kama***', desire, in every meaning of the word, in the service of liberation . . . not to sacrifice this world for liberation's sake, but to reinstate it, in varying ways, within the perspective of liberation."[8]

Some authors consider Bengal and Assam to have been the origin of ***Shakta*** and Tantric practices. At any rate, the Kamakhya temple in Assam and the Kalighat temple in Calcutta are among the most famous sacred places of Tantrism. A study of the religious geography of Tantrism would indicate that Shaktism and Hindu Tantrism were spread over the whole of India, and especially in the North-West, Kerala and the Bengal region.[9] In fact, we have seen that according to Payne the greatest hold of ***Shakta*** worship has been in the *Bengal* region.[10]

The "Debate" up to 1857

At the outset, let us recall that in the definition of Tantrism the *left-handed* practices are crucial: it is the performance of the "five m's" that has given Tantrism its risque flavour, in the eyes of the orthodox.

At the same time, we have noted that Tantrism lies at the very "core" of the Hindu tradition.[11] To take an example, almost all the temples in India have strong Tantric "elements" in their local traditions.[12] Thus, in the daily worship of Jagannath in Puri, the right-handed version of the Tantric ***panchatattva*** is offered to the deity: the "fifth m" (viz. ***maithuna***) is in the form of the dance of ***devadasis*** (until very recently) and the offering of ***aparajita*** flowers.[13]

Tantrism thus straddles the great traditions-little traditions dichotomy. As Padoux puts it, "Despite (its) autochthonous and perhaps 'popular' roots . . . Tantrism cannot be considered a popular form of religion in contrast to a 'higher' non-Tantric Hinduism."[14] And, even in modern times, there are localized left-handed activities based on the Tantric texts, though most people who talk about them have never actually seen them performed.[15]

The "Debate" in the Pan-Indian Culture

It is a truism that Hinduism is a most heterogeneous cultural phenomenon. The various elements of the Hindu tradition have borrowed from each other interminably, and created a rich cultural mix. For example, through the course of Indian history, pre-Aryan deities were assimilated to similar ***Brahman*** ones. In anthropological terms, little-tradition deities have continuously merged into the great-tradition pantheon.[16] Thus, the local goddess becomes assimilated to the great-tradition Durga.

In the reverse direction, pre-Aryan Indian culture gradually modified the patrifocal notions of the Aryans. The pre-Aryan culture was full of the worship of the mother-goddess; and this autochthonous element probably contributed to the salient dictum of the Hindu Tantrics, viz. "***Shivah shaktivihinah shavah***", i.e. "Shiva without Shakti is a corpse".[17]

Thus, Suniti Kumar Chatterjee and others have held the view that *woman* was the active partner in love-play in pre-Aryan India, and also even today in regions like Assam and Kerala which have been the stronghold of the Tantric tradition."[18] This pre-Aryan notion that the woman had to initiate courtship probably led to the concept of the ***abhisarika,*** which is influential in Indian poetics even today. This is a "reversal of the ***Vedic*** and Epic tradition".[19]

In short, the orthodox traditions of Indian religiosity teach asceticism as a pre-requisite to reach the goal of ***moksha,*** defined as the experience of ***samadhi*** (or "enstasy": vide Eliade, p. 37 et passim). There has been, however, a strong heterodox tradition of non-ascetical, erotic teachings which are older than Brahminical orthodoxy, and which probably came from the pre-Aryan culture. The ***Vedic*** elements thus came to stand for the exoteric aspects of the Indian tradition, while the non-***Vedic*** esoteric elements became heretical. According to the orthodox, enstasy — Mircea Eliade's term for the mystical experience — was to be reached by following the traditional canonical lore, and not by supererogatory methods. Even the methods of Patanjali ***yoga*** have been viewed with suspicion by the orthodox, despite the fact that classical ***yoga*** fell in line with the ascetical tradition.[20]

The anti-ascetical tradition, viz. the Tantric tradition, goes against the grain of orthodox Hinduism and is of bad repute. The Tantras are dangerous and heretical to the orthodox.[21] The flavour of these texts is definitely anti-Brahmanical, if not anti-caste. In them, one of the ***pashas*** or "fetters" binding the ordinary person is conformism, i.e. fear of social opinion. Most people, according to the ***vamacharins,*** thus actually shy away from left-handed practice because they are ***pashus,*** ("animals"), i.e. they conform to the non-Tantric, orthodox (i.e. ***Vedic***) observance.[22] The ***Brahmans*** are the main targets of the Tantrics' ***pashu*** - talk, because the former monopolize ***Vedic*** ritual, decide what is orthodox, and deny non-twice-born seekers access to the spiritual goals.[23] To the orthodox, of course, the *Tantric* is the ***pashu,*** because he does not control his senses; for the orthodox, ***Vamachara*** is a term of *abuse.*[24]

This centuries-old "debate" between the Tantrics and the establishment is very stereotyped. The Tantrics' argument is that in the ***Kaliyuga*** the canonical methods are not effective, and so a shorter route to salvation is needed. That is why the Tantric methods are, regrettably, necessary. The orthodox refute the Tantrics' claim that *liberation can be obtained through indulgence in the senses.* They say that the Tantric texts have no scriptural authority, and that their claim to being religious is hypocritical.[25] The Tantrics' *reply* to this criticism is that one does not have to go through the rigours of their training simply in order to enjoy wine and sexual intercourse.[26]

In short, the Tantrics' rationale for their praxis is that, unlike the teachings of the official culture, the senses must be stimulated to their *highest* pitch, so as to power the quest for enstasy.[27]

On the other hand, though the Tantrics claimed to be above societal morality—which is another reason why they attracted society's ire during the last fifteen centuries — their own texts pay lip-service to the orthodox, ascetical practices. This was probably done to make their practices more acceptable to their potential audience.[28]

To pacify the orthodox, the Tantrics used different stratagems. For one thing, they adopted orthodox ritual forms, including the use of purely ***Vedic mantras*** sometimes. In line with this, they also constantly asserted the conformity of Tantric with ***Vedic*** injunctions.[29] Further, they *concede* that though their method is a short-cut to liberation, it is dangerous and radical.[30]

All these apologetics evidence the marginal nature of Tantrism in the conservative Indian culture. Throughout the centuries, Indian views about women have remained basically unchanged. The basic axiom has been that woman's proper place is the home. Woman as lover or thinker or other autonomous person is not appreciated.[31]

The Tantric tradition did not really effect much change in this state of affairs. Even though the woman initiate has equal status with men in the ritual situation, she cannot maintain that status outside it. Further, the Tantric texts also echo the patriarchal ideology, because they make *low*-caste women the best ritual partners; this is a reflection of the general feeling that low-caste women are less inhibited, because more "sinful".[32]

In other words, the male Tantric is prey to a basic confusion about the role of women. On the one hand, he exalts her as the representative of the Goddess; on the other, *outside* the ritual situation, she is a second-class citizen.[33]

This identity-confusion of the Tantrics-in-society can be seen in their code-language called ***sandhabhasha,*** which consists of erotic terms that could be interpreted literally or metaphorically by the adept. They used this language to keep the Tantric teachings secret for a long time.[34] On the other hand, it has also been argued that they sometimes used this "intentional language" or ***sandhabhasha*** in a facetious manner, to annoy and tease the orthodox who constantly attacked them.[35]

That is to say, they resented and yet cherished their being "illicit", like mystics elsewhere.[36] This behaviour-syndrome is similar to Gluckman's "rites of rebellion", or Norbeck's "rites of reversal".[37] As Dumont rightly points out, the left-handed ***pancatattva*** ritual is a "sacramental enjoyment of all that is forbidden or despised in ordinary life"; it represents a "reversal of values".[38]

Still, though Tantrism has been in some sense heretical, the fact remains that it has *pervaded* Indian art, and has also survived in popular religion, according to Bolle. He points out that the Tantric aspects of the Hindu tradition are reflected in the marvellous works of temple art, which are "documents of a living tradition". They are evidence of Hinduism's "openness to the world, its love for the most beautiful and sensual."[39]

Padoux echoes this view: "far from being exceptional, Tantrism was in fact very widespread and indeed the common property of all the religions of 'medieval' India".[40] Thus he points out that the element of joy and playfulness (***lila***), which is one of the main elements of the Tantric world-view, may also be found in the non-Tantric context. It is particularly important in the Krishna cults, and is "one of the fields where Tantrism and ***'bhakti'*** meet".[41]

We come thus to the erotic religious sculpture of India, at Khajuraho, Konarak, and many other places. This forms the "extra-religious parameter" of Tantrism. In traditional Hinduism, man and woman are seen as representing the cosmic polarity. Thus "human sexuality is the mundane reflection of cosmic procreation".[42] The Hindu mystic, therefore, sees the union between the male and female principles as the union of Shiva and Shakti. Accordingly, in the ***shilpa-shastra,*** the principle of ***drishti-shuddhi*** (or "purity of gaze") requires that the outer walls of a temple have scenes from all aspects of everday life, including scenes of sexual coupling. The true worshipper is one who can see the numinous in everything, and especially in the most intimate experiences of life. Then, when he enters the sanctum, he worships the ***lingam,*** which is itself really a symbol of *renunciation,* since "renunciation is the acquisition of complete desirelessness: the orgasmic moment being the unique instance of complete desirelessness and complete fulfilment in human life. . .".[43]

In sum, though Tantrism has always been a matter of small groups— "of active minorities", to quote Louis Renou—it has had an enormous impact on "all Indian religions".[44] Tantric texts, temples, works of art, etc., continued to be produced right up to the eighteenth century, bearing witness to the vitality of this tradition. In its later phases, more and more of the texts began to come from "Brahmanic official circles". This may be proof of an increasing hold of Tantrism on the traditional centres of Hindu culture and learning".[45] In this context, we may recall that the great ***Adi***-Shankaracharya has traditionally been linked with ***devi***-worship. His connection with Tantrism cannot of course be definitely settled, but what is important for anthropologists is the traditional *perception* of him as a votary of Shakti.[46] Thus, it is quite plain that the "cultural debate" around Tantrism took place at the very *core* of the Hindu tradition.

The "Debate" in the Bengali Sub-culture

We have already seen that Tantrism, though spread over the whole of India, was especially popular in regions like *Bengal.* Bengal has long been especially receptive to the Tantric tradition. So much so that the Tantric ***Charyapadas*** are the earliest record of the Bengali language, dating to around a thousand years ago.

In the early period the local, royal courts were often patrons of Tantric cults, as we have seen, and this is an indicator of the dominant position of the movement. Later on, even during the Vaishnavite revival of the fourteenth and fifteenth centuries, Tantrism continued to retain its vitality. The influences of Vaishnavism, however, moulded the attitudes of ***Shakta*** Tantrics, who used ***Vaishnava*** themes to express the tender emotions of ***devi-bhakti.***

In the late-seventeenth and eighteenth centuries, there was a great revival of Tantrism. This was partly due to the revolt, in eighteenth-century Bengal, from the rarefied spirituality of the ***Vaishnavas.***[47] There was, nevertheless, a harmony between the two sects, as Ramprasad and his followers emphasized the essential identity of Kali and Krishna. This attitude was especially maintained by the later Tantric poets and thinkers, particularly from the middle of the eighteenth-century, partly to mollify the ***Vaishnavas*** who were provoked by the new custom of worshipping Kali publicly with great pomp.

In this connection, it may be noted that Kali, who is extremely popular in Bengal, may be worshipped by low-caste priests. As for ***Durga-puja,*** which has been the "national" festival of Bengal, it included, till late-medieval times, primitive elements like the celebration of ***Shabarotsava;*** this latter feast consisted of the performance of sexual songs and actions, in the presence of young women and also prostitutes.[48]

Given this *pervasive* nature of Tantrism in Bengal, it is not really surprising that even the ***Vaishnava*** movement inaugurated by Chaitanya was influenced by the (Tantric) ***Sahajiya*** tradition. We have seen that Chaitanya *himself* was quite possibly open to ***Sahajiya*** influences, partly because two of his early companions had links with that tradition; the wife of one of them, Jahnavi Devi, was herself a ***Sahajiya*** leader, and she was greatly respected as both the wife of Nityananda and as his spiritual successor.[49]

The distinction between orthodox ***Vaishnavas*** and the ***Sahajiya-Vaishnavas*** was thus not very important, even to people like the Gosvamis of Vrindavana, who were the theologians of Chaitanya's movement. It is thus recorded that Jahnavi-Devi was treated with great respect by them.[50] In point of fact, it is quite certain that the Gosvamis themselves were greatly influenced by the Tantras. Even though the Tantrism that influenced them was probably of the right-handed type, its "doctrinal and social position" had quite a lot in common with the left-handed Tantrism of the ***Sahajiyas.*** The latter were thus able, in fact, to use the Gosvamis as authorities to justify their *own* position.[51]

Of course, to the orthodox the ***Vaisnava-Sahajiyas*** were not, for obvious reasons, fully respectable. Orthodox ***Vaishnavas*** cannot accept, for example, that theories about the nature of their beloved Gauranga or Chaitanya (for instance, the theory of his dual incarnation as Radha and Krishna) may have been influenced by the ***Sahajiya*** viewpoint. The fact still remains, however, that pre-Chaitanya ***Sahajiya*** doctrine quite possibly influenced both Bengali Vaishnavite theology and thoughts about Chaitanya himself. Indeed, some ***Sahajiya*** texts go so far as to try to show that Chaitanya himself was a ***Sahajiya*** ![52]

The truth probably is that the two traditions influenced

each other mutually. Some of the ***Vaishnava*** ideas, like the dual incarnation of Chaitanya, were probably derived from the long-existing ***Sahajiya*** tradition. On the other hand, Vaishnavism provided the ***Sahajiyas*** with a ready-made theology, which they of course reinterpreted.[53]

In short, the Tantric tradition was very intimately interwoven into the texture of Bengali culture, through the centuries that preceded the period that concerns us here. Let us, therefore, turn now to the situation in Bengal between 1857 and 1947.

The "Debate" in Modern Bengal, 1857 to 1947

According to Bharati, the main characteristic of modern Hinduism is its "puritanism";[54] this urban, official Hinduism is very hostile to hedonistic and sensual values. Starting from about three hundred years ago, and largely due to the British impact on India, Hinduism has cut its links with the healthy sensuality that was at its core, and that is represented by Khajuraho and suchlike cultural artifacts.[55] This increasing puritanism is evidenced in the recent trend, started by Swami Dayanand and others, to worship Shiva anthropomorphically; traditionally, he has been worshipped in the ***linga*** form, which has, however, no conscious erotic implications for the orthodox.[56] In the case of Krishna also, this puritanism has led to the de-emphasis of his persona as lover, and the emphasis of the sexless protagonist of the *Bhagavad Gita.*

Bharati argues, therefore, that this is the reason why the erotica that covers Indian temple walls, at Khajuraho and other places, still troubles modern Indians, who have deeply internalized the ideology of the British missionaries and administrators.[57] They condemn these works as obscene; in fact, Gandhi even wished that they could be dismantled, as we saw earlier in Chapter II.

The official, urban culture of India thus rejects the Tantric tradition outright.[58] The Tantric teaching that the religious goals can be attained through "controlled *sensual* indulgence"[59] is anathema to this official *weltanschaung.* For example, Swami Dayanand wrote a separate chapter in his *"Satyartha Prakash"* to denounce it.[60] During the last few decades, whenever organized left-handed practice has become known, the reactions have been extremely hostile. For instance, the Kutchi "Om Mandali", a religious sect which was involved in some sort of left-handed practice, had its headquarters raided by the police in the early 1950's.[61]

We may not agree with *all* aspects of Bharati's above polemic. Still, the reactions of Western scholars towards Tantrism during the period under consideration were largely negative, and Bengali intellectuals tended to *echo* these sentiments. So much so that Sivacandra Vidyarnava claimed that he composed his *"Tantrattva"* (which Woodroffe published under the title, *"Principles of Tantra"*) in order to *rebut* the English tracts written by Englishmen and by English-educated Bengalis, which gave a distorted picture of Tantrism.[62] We can conclude, therefore, that the British influence—which provided the *external* input to the "cultural debate", as per Parkin's model—at the very least strongly *reinforced* the centuries-old diatribe against Tantrism, during the period we are studying.

Let us now look specifically at the so-called *"pizza -effect"* aspect of the external input to the "debate". We may recall that this refers to the phenomenon of Indians, during the past one hundred years or so, becoming interested in items of their culture, once these were appreciated by Western thinkers and scholars. This phenomenon is also increasingly evident in regard to the erotic aspects of Indian culture, it would appear. Thus, some members of the intelligentsia have come to *accept* the "erotic-esoteric" part of the tradition, and this small vocal group of Hindus has an increasing audience, which has even begun to appreciate the erotic sculptures of Khajuraho, etc.[63]

As to whether, however, the *pizza-effect* has had a more direct impact on the "cultural debate" around Tantrism, the evidence is rather negative. It is certainly true that Woodroffe's efforts to promote Tantrism were rewarded with some success. Thus, although a great number of Tantric texts had been edited in India by the end of the nineteenth century, his *"Tantrik Texts Series"* became known to a *wider* public than just the devotees and admirers of Tantrism. At any rate, it opened up the field of Tantrism to scholars.[64]

In spite of Woodroffe, however, Tantric studies are still only incipient. Indian scholars who study Tantrism, like Benoytosh Bhattacharya, S.B. Dasgupta and Chintaharan Chakravarti—incidentally, all three are Bengalis—*still* do so with an air of apology. In other words, though the *pizza-effect* has been operative during the last one hundred years as regards the erotic aspects of Indian culture also, it has *not* been that much in evidence vis-a-vis the "debate" around *Tantrism*. It would seem that the erotic is still rather taboo as a part of Indian religion and philosophy.[65]

Let us next see what the attitudes of India's *traditional* groups were towards Tantrism, during our period of focus. The attitude of traditional Hindus, and of modern Hindus exposed to Western learning — as opposed to that of the alienated "official" group — was ambiguous. Some of them, *mainly Bengalis*, have displayed sympathy for Tantrism. Thus, the outstanding Tantric scholar Mm. Gopinath Kaviraj was an apologist for Tantrism. Like other Tantrics since the early decades of the twentieth century, he tried to show that Tantrism is really a ***Vedic*** praxis. This is done in order to make left-handed practice more palatable to the orthodox and puritanical establishment.[66]

Some non-Tantric pundits also do of course have an open mind with regard to the Tantrics' claim that their ***sadhana*** is a fit one for the present ***Kaliyuga***. They are aware that all formal non-***Vedic*** ritual conducted by women and by non-***Brahmin*** villagers is Tantric. In general, the orthodox in Kerala, Orissa, Assam and *Bengal* (all traditional strongholds of Tantrism) tend to be lenient towards left-handed practice. In fact, the term ***Shakta*** tends to be somewhat charismatic in Assamese and *Bengali*. It is to be noted, however, that both Tantrics and their sympathizers warn of the great dangers involved in left-handed methods.[67]

The main apologetic used by modern Tantrics is that, since religious texts have accepted sexual enjoyment for all beings — the *"Kama Shastras"* are in fact semi-*canonical* texts—their performance of the "five m's" is really a *worship* of the goddess. They quote non-Tantric sources which support their view, e.g. the story of Mohini, that of Parvati's seduction of Shiva (which led to the birth of Kumara), and the famous passage in the ***"Brihadaranyaka Upanishad"*** which narrates how a woman should be courted and made love to. Of course, the orthodox assume that the *Upanishad* refers to a married couple; the Tantric reply to this is that their consecration of a Shakti is of a higher order than the ***Vedic*** marriage ceremony, and that in any case its acceptance by society does not matter to them.[68]

We may also note at this juncture that some of the greatest figures of that period had ambiguous, if not positive, attitudes in the debate around Tantrism. As regards Rammohan Roy, Debendranath Tagore records (though somewhat sceptically) the claim of a Tantric ***sannyasi*** whom he met in Delhi in 1857, that Roy was a Tantric disciple of Swami Hariharanandanatha.[69] Moreover, the association of Roy with the ***"Mahanirvana*** Tantra" was so close[70] that Debendranath adapted material from it to compose one of the finest hymns used in the services of the christianized ***Brahmo Samaj.***[71]

More significantly, Ramakrishna himself was *directly* involved with left-handed praxis at one time, though later on both he and the Ramakrishna Mission played down this aspect of his ***sadhana.*** Nevertheless, his influence was very much evident in Vivekananda's and Keshab Chunder Sen's references to God as Mother. Then there is Rabindranath Tagore's link with the (Tantric) Bauls. Further, we may notice that Aurobindo's ***Yoga*** system had also many Tantric elements. And finally, it has also been observed that the revival of Shaktism and the Indian Nationalist Movement mutually influenced each other in this period, as we shall see later in Chapter 6.

Conclusion: Bengali Attitudes Towards Tantrism, 1857 to 1947

We thus come to the end of our argument. We have seen that the focus of the *cultural debate* around Tantrism, through the centuries, was the belief that passions jeopardize the quest for ***moksha,*** which belief was of course rejected by the Tantrics. And the official culture of India in modern times has *reinforced* this basic conservatism of Indian society in the "debate" around Tantrism. This process has, in great measure, also been helped by the *external* input to the "debate", as represented by the British rule in India.

As regards the so-called *pizza-effect* dimension of the external participation in the "debate", this has really been evident only in regard to the more *secular* aspects of the Indian erotic tradition; as part of the religious, however, the erotic is still taboo. Still, some of my own *Bengali* ***Brahman*** informants in Assam, during the last few years, spoke *approvingly* of the efforts of Woodroffe: here was a British Judge of the Calcutta High Court, no less, who had found it worth his while to investigate their esoteric Tantric tradition. On the other hand, however, traditional groups in the matrifocal areas of India, like Kerala, Orissa, Assam and *Bengal,* have also tended to be less hostile towards Tantrism. This is due to the continuities in the centuries-old "debate" around this theme. When they warn of the dangers inherent in Tantric praxis, they do so only in terms of "mental derangement, and less so in terms of "spiritual downfall".[72]

Of course, we have also noted that the attitudes of the establishment in *Bengal* during this period have been quite ambivalent, due to the *strong* Tantric component in the Bengali sub-culture. Thus, Aurobindo's system of ***yoga*** would have been "unthinkable without the Tantric tradition", and it also shows the *persistence* of Tantrism, which has been able to find "new forms of expression in modern times".[73] This persistent Tantric under-current has been responsible, in fact, for the comparative liberalism of Bengali culture even today.[74]

We may, therefore, safely conclude that social attitudes in the Bengal region continued to be generally *supportive,* and Tantrism *continued* to hold its own in the "culrural debate" around it, during the period from 1857 to 1947.

References

1. This Chapter, and the following one, are based on the author's M.A. paper, written at the University of Pennsylvania in 1987 under the supervision of Prof. Arjun Appadurai
2. *Cf.* Parkin
3. *Ibid,* pp. 291-292
4. *Ibid*
5. Bharati (1981), p. 21, n. 3
6. *Ibid*
7. Gupta et al, pp. 5-9
8. Padoux, pp. 273
9. Gupta et al, pp. 36-39
10. *Cf.* Payne
11. Bharati (1978 : 168)
12. Bharati (1976a : 85)
13. Bhattacharya (1982 : 375)
14. Padoux, p. 275
15. Bharati (1978 : 168-169)
16. Bharati (1976a : 220)
17. *Ibid,* pp. 202-205
18. *Ibid,* p. 224, n. 2
19. *Ibid,* p. 206
20. *Ibid,* pp. 286-289
21. *Ibid,* p. 289
22. *Ibid,* pp. 233-235
23. *Ibid,* p. 242
24. *Ibid,* pp. 240-242
25. Bharati (1978 : 169-170)
26. *Ibid,* p. 170
27. Bharati (1976a : 290)
28. *Ibid,* pp. 289-290
29. *Ibid,* pp. 240-246
30. *Ibid,* p. 21.
31. Bharat (1964 : 149-154)
32. *Ibid*
33. *Ibid,* p. 161
34. Bharat (1978 : 290)
35. *Ibid,* pp. 171-172
36. Bharati (1977 : 206)
37. Bharati (1976b), Vol. 2, p. 3
38. Dumont, pp. 278-282
39. Bolle, (1965), Foreword, pp. XIV to XV
40. Padoux, p. 273
41. *Ibid,* p. 277
42. Bharati (1978), 189-190 et passim
43. *Ibid,* pp. 330-331
44. Padoux, p. 274
45. *Ibid,* p. 275
46. Bharati (1981 : 34)

47. Payne, p. 94
48. Bhattacharya (1974 : 134-145)
49. Dimock, (1966 : 121)
50. *Ibid*
51. *Ibid*, p. 83
52. *Ibid*, pp. 37-39
53. *Ibid*, pp. 39-40
54. Bharati (1971 : 100)
55. Bharati (1981 : 17-18)
56. Bharati (1978 : 175-176)
57. *Ibid*, p. 300
58. *Ibid*, p. 171
59. *Ibid*, p. 30
60. *Ibid*, p. 171
61. *Ibid*, p. 172
62. Bhattacharya (1982), Introduction, p. 30
63. Bharati (1978 : 171)
64. Payne, p. 3
65. Bharati (1976a), Preface, pp. 9-10
66. Bharat (1978 : 173-175)
67. *Ibid*
68. Bharati (1976a : 242-243)
69. *Cf.* Killingley
70. Suniti Kumar Chatterjee, in Ray, p. 37
71. Payne, p. 98
72. Bharati (1978 : 175)
73. Bolle (1965), Foreword, p. XVI
74. Dasgupta, p. 76

6

Tantrism and the "Hindu Renaissance" in Bengal

TANTRISM has been neglected till quite recently, as we have seen. It was Sir John Woodroffe's work at the beginning of this century that helped to make it respectable, despite which, however, serious Tantric studies are still only beginning. In this chapter, I propose to examine social attitudes to Tantrism vis-a-vis the *"Hindu Renaissance"* in Bengal.

The main heuristic tool I have used here is Agehananda Bharati's novel use of the term "Hindu Renaissance", which is "in conscious contrast to earlier uses" of it, as he puts it.[1] In the usual usage, the term refers to the revival of interest among Indians in their traditional culture, which was sparked by the interest in Indian culture evinced by European Indologists and which stimulated the English-educated intelligentsia, especially in Bengal.

Bharati uses the term, however, to refer to the brand of Hinduism espoused by the *alienated* urbanite, which is quite different from *traditional* Hinduism.[2] His usage refers to the "totality of puritanical, ascetical-antiesthetical pattern of modern Hindu ideas . . .".[3] According to him, this revival began in the early days of the British Raj, and peaked around the time of Indian Independence.[4] Bharati's usage (which I shall distinguish by putting it within quotation marks, viz. "Hindu Renaissance") provides us a method to get at the attitudes towards Tantrism of the Bengali *intelligentsia* during this colonial period.

Let us now look more closely at Bharati's description of his term "Hindu Renaissance": it is based on the *simplistic* teachings of Vivekananda and other ***gurus*** and leaders.[5] He feels that these teachings were derived from the Christian missionaries who taught them English.[6] This led to a kind of "Christianized Hinduism", which is highly puritanical, and which resulted in modern Hindus being alienated from the more matter-of-fact attitude of the grassroots Hindu tradition towards the male-female relationship.[7] For example, the Victorian attitudes of the British missionaries and administrators, such as their notions about obscenity, were directly transferred to reformers like Rammohan Roy, Keshab Sen, Swami Vivekananda, and to politicians like Mohandas Gandhi.[8] Thus, we have already seen that Gandhi wished that he had the power to pull down the erotica on the walls of the temples of Khajuraho ! [9]

Let us then turn to the situation in Bengal. Throughout the nineteenth and the early twentieth century, it led the rest of the country. It was the biggest and most populated province of British India. Being the first area to come under British rule, it was ahead of the other regions in English education. It had the most newspapers and periodicals, for instance. Calcutta was developing in this period into one of the world's important seaports. This revitalization of Bengali life has often been called the "Bengal Renaissance".[10]

The high-caste elite entered the professions and government, besides being most often the largest landowners. In 1931, they formed only about six per cent of the population of Bengal, but almost thirty-one per cent of that of Calcutta. It may also be pointed out here that most of them were ***Shaktas.***[11]

Gradually, with every passing generation, this Bengali intelligentsia experienced an "ambivalence of religious identity", which grew more and more intense. This ambivalence was visible as early as 1800. Reformers like Ram Ram Basu (an intimate of William Carey's) attacked the social and religious evils of Hinduism with "an evangelical indignation", which has a strange middle-class tone to it. The "Christian-inspired puritanical attacks on the twin evils of moral laxity and idolatry" were later institutionalized by Rammohan Roy and Debendranath Tagore in the ***Brahmo*** movement. In Ram Ram Basu, we see the first stage in the "invention" of a monotheistic tradition in Hinduism.[12]

In Ram Ram's existential situation we can recognize the personality structures of many members of the Bengali intelligentsia of the nineteenth century. Of all these, Rammohan Roy seems to be Ram Ram's real successor. These Bengalis invited the contempt of the traditionalists for their reformist activities, and experienced a growing cultural alienation and marginality.[13] As Gunderson puts it, "Nineteenth century Bengali culture had many Victorian characteristics, and not a few of its deficiencies. There was a lack of interest in things if they were not immediately useful."[14]

Of all the leaders of the Bengal Renaissance, Rammohan Roy is the most famous. He has been "thoroughly integrated into the cultural self-image of the (Bengali) people". His charisma has so influenced historians that the beginning of the Indian Ranaissance has often been dated from the year 1815, when he settled in Calcutta. According to Kopf, he contributed powerfully to the "puritanization" of the Hindu tradition in Bengal.[15]

Rammohan's Contribution Significant

Rammohan's conception of "the theistic ***Brahmo,*** the cornerstone of his reformation movement", was very likely based on the published work of Ram Ram Basu.[16] Rammohan's contribution to the "Hindu Renaissance" is significant. His view of the Hindu tradition is an interesting one; he fought for what he believed was the cultural purification of Hinduism, and the monotheistic theology of the ***Brahmo Samaj*** was basic to his view of authentic Hinduism.[17]

Roy's Brahmo Sabha was the precursor of the ***Brahmo Samaj.*** These organizations were based on his views about ***Vedic*** Hinduism. His basic idea that "all major religions had similar traditions in spite of diversity of form became the universalist credo of the ***Samaj***". He could not, however, resolve the conflict between the "universality of mankind and the psychological need to maintain one's Hindu identity"; this conflict led to the later split in the ***Samaj,*** between Keshub Sen and Debendranath Tagore.[18]

There is, however, *another* aspect of Rammohan's career that is especially relevant to us, in that it specifically concerns his relationship to Tantrism. As Suniti Kumar Chatterji puts it, "he had made a study of Tantra . . ." and it was said that he even followed some (left-handed) Tantra practices.[19] Niharranjan Ray also points to his close association with the (Tantric) ***avadhut*** Hariharananda Swami . . . and his regard for the "***Mahanirvana*** Tantra" in particular.[20] Rammohan's "acceptance" of Tantra may in fact have been due to the traditional "liberalism in Bengal's religious thoughts and practices . . . (which can) be traced to Tantra to some extent . . .", according to Dasgupta.[21] Perhaps it was also because he was impressed by Tantra's liberal attitudes towards caste, marriage, ***"suttee"*** and other practices, and also because he felt that the main strains of Tantra ran parallel with Vedanta.[22]

Turning from Roy, we come to another famous member of the Bengali intelligentsia in this period, namely, Bankimchandra Chatterji. He was the first graduate of Calcutta University, and in his articles and novels he gave voice to the orthodox party, which was still strong. In his ***"Krishnacharita"*** he attacked Christianity, comparing Krishna and Christ to the latter's disadvantage.[23] Bankim felt that English education was rapidly destroying Indian culture; he stressed that English values were not necessarily good for Indians.[24] In his later novels like ***"Ananda Math"*** he extolled Kali as the goddess of the Hindus; his hymn to Kali, **"Bande Mataram,"** became the slogan of the early nationalists.[25]

He was, however, *inimical* to Tantrism. In 1860 he once met a ***Kapalik*** at Neguan; the latter was the prototype of the ***Kapalik*** in Bankim's novel ***"Kapalkundala".*** He gave this character the most repulsive features, showing clearly his attitude to Tantrism which he saw as "one of the ugliest and (most) fearsome vestiges of the Middle Ages". Many years later, in his polemics with Hastie regarding Hinduism, he referred to this novel in which he had expressed his "strong disapproval" of this part of Hinduism. In other words, Bankim, who was supposedly the voice of the orthodox party in this period, was extremely hostile to Tantrism; in contrast his precursor Rammohan, though the leader of the reformists, was more accepting of the Tantric tradition.

The reform movements, like Rammohan Roy's, however, affected *only* the English-educated intelligentsia; they had very little influence on the majority of Indians, who were rural. The intelligentsia were, however, also affected by the interest in Indian culture evinced by European Indologists. As a result, English-educated Indians strangely began to offer "scientific" interpretations of all aspects of Hinduism.[26] In that period of eclecticism, the poet Hemchandra Bandyopadhyay, in his famous poem, **"Dasha-mahavidya"**, tried to correlate the Tantric ***"Dasha-Mahavidyas"*** with the theory of evolution.[27]

At the same time, well-known nineteenth-century writers like Michael Madhusudhan Dutta, who had become a Christian and then lapsed into being a free-thinker,[28] composed many ***Shakta*** lyrics, of which his poem "Vijaya" is an excellent example. Kamalakanta Bhattacharya popularized the Tantric teachings; his ***"Sadhakaranjana"*** explains the basic principles of the Tantras in simple verse. The tradition of the ***Shakta*** ***"Mangalakavyas"*** was also maintained, for example by the romantic poet Biharilal Chakravarty.[29]

Also, ***Durga Puja,*** the great autumnal festival of the goddess, maintained its hold on the public. Michael Madhusudhan Dutta's beautiful poem "Vijaya", mentioned above, was in the tradition of the ***Vijaya*** (farewell) songs, which depict the mother's (and Menaka's) feelings when the daughter (Durga) returns to her husband's home.[30] Thus, ***Durga Puja*** remained the Bengali "national festival".[31] This festival, though popular all over India, is celebrated with especial enthusiasm in Eastern India, particularly Bengal.[32]

In this connection, it may be mentioned that the famous ***Shakta*** Tantric text, the ***Kalikapurana***, has been frequently used in the ***Durga Puja*** ceremonies. It was popular among Sanskrit writers from the fourteenth century on, and was used as a guide during ***Durga Puja*** rituals in Bengal and Assam;[33] in fact, according to Dr Sanjukta Gupta, it is still used for this purpose.[34] Incidentally the *Kalikapurana* was notorious among European scholars for the human sacrifice described in one of its chapters,[35] but these sensational rites form only a minor part of its rituals.[36] Of more relevance to our topic, this important text mentions, in connection with the ***Durga Puja*** festival, the feast of ***Shabarotsava***"[37] This feast of the late-medieval, and even recent times, involved the singing of sexual songs and the miming of sexual actions, as the Durga image was taken for immersion.[38]

Ramakrishna Offers Simple Vision of Hinduism

Then, in this period, there was also another group of ***Shaktas*** who were more concerned with religious praxis than with the Tantric texts. Many of these were illiterate; of these, mention may be made of Sarvananda in Tripura, Gosain Bhattacharya in Dacca, and the female ***Shakta*** saint Jayadurga or Ardhakali in Mymensingh who was believed to be the Divine Mother herself. And then there was the famous Ramakrishna, who fitted in this tradition of popular Bengali ***Shakta*** saints; he provided a very broad and simple vision of Hinduism, to meet the ideological needs of the common people in the rapidly changing circumstances.[39]

Ramakrishna was a powerful figure of the "Hindu Renaissance". He was a part of the popular movement of Shaktism, which had been evolving since the time of Ramprasad in the eighteenth century. He joined the worship of Kali to an eclectic belief in the equivalence of all religions. He became popular among the educated middle-class of Calcutta, from whom most of his disciples came. These disciples, led by Vivekananda, seized upon such simplistic beliefs and powerfully expounded them as the *essence* of Hinduism.

On the other hand, Ramakrishna had been very much involved with left-handed Tantric practice at one stage of his life. Thus, though he was often antagonistic to Tantrism later on, he also on occasion made statements that were quite *sympathetic.*[40] At any rate, Ramakrishna's Tantric experimentation involved a handsome ***Bhairavi*** (i.e. female worshipper of ***Shakti***), in her late thirties. Guided by her, he undertook his Tantric ***sadhana*** between 1861 and 1863. According to his prime biographer, his Tantric experience supposedly proved that Tantrism "could be practised in compete chastity." Later Ramakrishna *did* admit that he was "once attacked by lust" (sic).[41]

The Ramakrishna Mission, quite understandably, downplayed this phase of the great man's career. For example, they projected the ***Bhairavi Brahmani's*** attitude towards him as putatedly one of "motherly affection". Apparently, the Divine Mother Herself took care to see him through the dangerous praxis safely, so that he did not "sink into moral degradation" (sic). In short, Ramakrishna is supposed to have introduced "an element of purity into the Tantrika practices"; and this was of course a sign of "the greatness of his character", in the eyes of his followers.[42]

Anyway, Ramakrishna was throughout his life influenced by ***Shakta*** ideas. His influence, in this regard, can also be traced on Keshub Chunder Sen and Swami Vivekananda, who were under quite strong Christian influence and "yet remained apologists for the worship of the Goddess.[43] Thus, the presence of ***Shakta*** ideas, probably mediated by Ramakrishna, can be seen in Vivekananda's and Keshub Sen's references to God as Mother.[44] Taking the case of Sen first, he had been of Vaishnavite bent, and at the same time, as a leader of the ***Brahmo Samaj,*** very receptive to Christian ideas. He came under the influence of Ramakrishna, and in October 1879 when Bengal was in the throes of ***Durga Puja***, he issued a proclamation on behalf of the ***Brahmo Samaj,*** in which he fervently spoke of the *Motherhood* of God.[45]

As for Vivekananda, Ramakrishna's favourite disciple, he visited the Baishno Devi Shrine in Kashmir in 1898, and thenceforth emphasized the worship of the Mother. He spoke of struggling for six years before finally accepting Her.[46] According to Sister Nivedita, he often said that he worshipped Kali "with her foot on the heart of the worshipper".[47] Nivedita also records that the songs of the great ***Shakta*** poet Ramprasad were often on Vivekananda's lips.[48]

The above attitudes of leading religious figures like Keshub Sen and Vivekananda were quite possibly a reaction to the Westernizing influences of the late-nineteenth century. The Mutiny of 1857 had been a revolt against British rule and Christianity, among other things, and the atrocities on both sides left deep scars. In the years following there were also disputes between European indigo planters and the exploited peasants, whose sufferings were depicted in Dina Bandhu Mitra's Bengali drama of 1860, ***Nil Darpan***.[49]

It was in this context that orthodox Hinduism began to be revived, and the educated began to clamour for self-government. The two phenomena were inter-related. Further, the rise in the cost of living affected the Bengali lower-middle classes (clerks, teachers, etc.), and they were the groups most receptive to ideas such as the revival of the cult of Kali.

This revival of the cult of Shakti played its part in the growth of Indian nationalism. From the middle of the nineteenth century, the Divine Mother was used as a symbol for India by many of the Bengali intelligentsia, among whom were Michael Madhusudhan Dutta and Aurobindo Ghose.[50] Conversely, the struggle between 1905 and 1911 for the revocation of the partition of Bengal helped in the revival of ***Shakta*** ideas. Kali was regarded as the "personification of the province of Bengal". Resistance to British rule acquired religious sanction.

Despite his own Vaishnavite convictions, Bankimchandra had in 1860 written his ***"Bande Mataram"*** hymn in his novel ***Ananda Math*** about the ***Sannyasi*** rebellion of the eighteenth century. This song became popular among the nationalists; the above novel moved the youth of Bengal, who were inspired by its story of a group of revolutionaries who dedicate themselves to the motherland, which they identified with the goddess Kali.[51] It is possible, of course, that Bankim was referring only to Kali in that famous song, and not to the country. Nevertheless, in 1906 Rabindranath sang it to his own music at the Calcutta session of the Indian National Congress.[52]

This revival of Shaktism became so popular that Surendranath Banerjee and other leaders encouraged the linking of Shakti and Kali with meetings in favour of ***"Swaraj"*** and ***"Swadeshi"***. It is an interesting pointer to the pervasive nature of ***Shakta*** ideas in Bengal then that, though the shouting of ***"Bande Mataram"*** in the streets had been proscribed in 1906, British officers stood up and sang it with the audience at a recruiting drive during the First World War.[53]

Aurobindo Ghose also started a monthly called *Bande Mataram* which he used as a vehicle for his idealistic views of the Mother.[54] Swami Vivekananda, who we have seen derived his ***Shakta***-oriented outlook from his master Ramakrishna, regarded the country as the living image of the Divine Mother. Even Rabindranath Tagore, who was otherwise hostile to the ***Shakta*** religious practices, reflected this tendency in his nationalist poems.[55] And, in the Bengal Press, a lot of material linked the great Goddess to the Motherland. Some of this popularity was also used by those of the nationalists who advocated the use of violent means of resistance; after Jallianwala Bagh, such groups used the figure of Kali to justify bloodshed.[56]

Tagore's Views on Tantrism

At this juncture, let us take a more detailed look at Rabindranath Tagore's views about Tantrism. At the outset, we may point out here that his Shantiniketan complex is situated near Tarapitha in the Birbhum district of modern West Bengal; this whole area is one in which the "Tantric tradition is ancient and all-pervasive", and where the Goddess is worshipped with ***Shakta*** ritual.[57] Tarapitha is also associated with the ***Shakta*** saint Vamacharana, popularly known as Vama-Kshepa.[58] Further, the area is inhabited by a large population of Santhals, a tribal people who are more extroverted and less inhibited in their interpersonal relations than the surrounding Hindus.[59]

Tagore was influenced by both ***Vaishnava*** and ***Shakta*** traditions.[60] It was he who made modern Bengalis see the Bauls as something other than "a laughing stock".[61] He praised their beautiful songs, and frankly acknowledged his literary debt to them. Again, Tagore's songs were also influenced by the poems of the Tantric Ramprasad.[62] Further, Sibnarayan Ray points out that it is possible to detect the echoes of the early-medieval ***Charya***-poems of the Tantric ***Siddhas*** in "the over-refined world of . . . (Tagore's) *Gitanjali*".[63] It is due to the influence of Tagore, and of the "aesthetic renascence" ushered in by him, that the Bengali intellectuals of this century are less puritanical than their counterparts in the rest of India.[64]

In reference to Tagore's link with the Bauls, it may be mentioned that it is quite possible that the (Tantric) ***Sahajiya*** cult is *still* followed secretly by them. As Dimock puts it, "There is an eternal borrowing of ideas and doctrines that . . . has always gone on among religious sects in India, until the lines of deviation become very blurred"; and the doctrines of the Bauls are very similar to those of the ***Sahajiyas,*** though the majority of Bauls cannot be called ***Sahajiyas.***[65] Padoux is even more explicit, in this regard; he says that the Bauls represent a "modern form" of the ***Vaishnava-Sahajiyas,*** "with their peculiar erotic mysticism . . ."[66] There are, in point of fact, many terms in the Baul songs that are specific to the Tantric tradition, and that refer to the ***chakras*** of the Tantric system of meditation.[67]

Before we leave the ***Sahajiyas,*** we may also notice the interesting fact that Mahatma Gandhi, who otherwise so exemplified the attitudes of the "Hindu Renaissance" (as we noted vis-a-vis his attitude towards the erotic sculptures at Khajurajo), practised an intriguing technique of ***brahmacharya*** or "celibacy". He tried to carry his conception of ***brahmacharya*** to a logical conclusion by "becoming a woman". He did this by sleeping nude with a naked young woman, without touching her sexually. We may note that this is the same technique employed by the ***Sahajiyas*** in their ***sadhana;***[68] as the anthropologist Nirmal Kumar Bose, who was Gandhi's secretary during that period, put it with scholarly understatement, this is rather "reminiscent of the Tantras".[69]

Aurobindo's "Integral Yoga" and Tantrism

Another important "Hindu Renaissance" figure who was influenced by Tantric ideas was Aurobindo Ghose. As Bolle remarks, "Crucial symbolisms in Aurobindo's (***Yoga***) system are of a Tantric character", despite his tedious urge for conceptualization, which was partly due to the fact that he wrote in English, into which language ***yogic*** concepts are difficult to translate.[70]

The basis of his system is the idea that both Matter and Spirit are real. This is a continuation of the old Tantric teachings. The characteristic Tantric equations of ***nirvana*** with ***samsara,*** and of ***mukti*** with ***bhukti,*** are congruent with this system. Of course, Tantric ideas underwent a transformation in it, due to India's exposure to the modern world, which caused Aurobindo to reinterpret the old teachings in order to accommodate a modern audience. Thus, for example, he posed the problem of physical existence in a more straightforward way which did not take the idea of ***samsara*** for granted.[71]

Again, his scheme of levels or planes of reality can be compared to the subtle physiology of the Hindu and Buddhist Tantras, with its system of ***chakras,*** etc. There is in both the Tantric system and in Aurobindo's the same urge for a "beyond beyond the beyond", i.e. no single ***chakra*** or level exhausts the Absolute. There is always a higher stage to be reached; and in both systems, there is no doubt expressed about the possibility of experiencing the highest levels.[72]

The very name of Aurobindo's system, viz. "Integral ***Yoga***", refers to this urge to incorporate all experience; this attitude is similar to that of Tantrism. Aurobindo himself points out that his system is an *elaboration* of the ***Shakta*** Tantra teachings, which to him are "broader and larger" than other systems of ***yoga;*** of course, the goal of *his* ***yoga*** is even higher than that of the Tantric unity of ***mukti*** and ***bhukti:*** it is the "perfect outflowering of the Divine in Humanity". And, like the Tantras, he claims that his system is the "shortest way" to the goal. In short, it is difficult to distinguish between the two symbolic systems: among other things, both use symbolism which is at once cosmological and individual.[73]

Let us finally look at the evidence of *direct* interest in Tantrism as such. In the nineteenth century, Western scholars of Indian religion, like H. H. Wilson and M. Monier-Williams, regarded Tantrism as a set of barbarous and obnoxious practices.[74] Again, A. Barth characterized the left-handed rites as "delirious mysticism", and called the left-handed ***Shakta*** "a hypocrite and a superstitious debauchee".[75] Thus, as Padoux remarks, Tantrism was for Western experts a very peculiar, even repulsive, aspect of Indian religion.[76] Goudriaan feels that this attitude was "possibly due to their Christian conditioning".[77] This reaction persisted well into the twentieth century, so that Payne wrote in 1933 that ***Shakta*** literature is "debasing", and that their spirituality is "no real excuse for the sensuality of much that is in the Tantras."[78]

Orthodox Hindu intellectuals—"sometimes under British influence", according to Goudriaan—also tended to see Tantrism as "a wilful breach" of the ***sanatana dharma.***[79] Thus, Bankimchandra Chatterji considered Tantrism to be a misguided involvement with wine and woman, under the guise of religion. Another Bengali, R. L. Mitra, also considered these practices revolting and depraved.[80] Even in the first half of the twentieth century, Benoytosh Bhattacharya, a pioneer in the study of ***Vajrayana,*** considered Tantrism a sign that the mind of the entire society was *diseased.* He pointed out that Tantrism had been left alone by scholars due to its repugnant contents; he sadly noted that the Hindus were still in the thrall of Tantrism in their daily life and in their customs. He not surprisingly felt, therefore, that the Hindu society should be cured of this disease.[81]

On the other hand, in the twentieth century the Tantras began to be seriously studied by Westerners. In 1900, Manmatha Nath Dutt's English translation of the '***Mahanirvana Tantra***' was published in Calcutta. From 1923 Woodroffe's *Tantrik Texts Series* was issued, and it was mainly his efforts that changed the attidudes of scholars towards the Tantras.[82] Thus, in 1921 Sir Charles Elliott felt that Tantric principles are liberal in that "caste restrictions are minimized . . . (and) women are honoured."[83]

According to Payne, partly as a result of the increasing contact with the West, many of the more dubious ***Shakta*** practices "disappeared, or were suppressed". Thus, Avalon (alias Woodroffe) referred in his books to the work of "several ***Shakta*** theologians, and . . . translated the ***'Tantrattava'*** or *"Principles of Tantra'*, written by one of them." Again, Bankimchandra described the practices of the ***Shaktas*** in several of his novels, of which ***Kapalkundala*** and ***Ananda Math*** are well known, as we have seen. Many beliefs connected with Shakti were revived in the twentieth century, and a popular literature developed around them.[84]

Coming to the traditional groups, Bengali aristocrats had shown a *renewed* interest in Tantrism, in the latter part of the eighteenth and the beginning of the nineteenth century. This had resulted in the writing of Tantric digests like the ***'Pranatoshini'*** and the ***'Haratattvavidhi'***.[85] Then, about a century ago, scholarly works on ***Shakta*** Tantrism began to be produced in the Bengali vernacular. Even though this falls outside the "creative period of Tantric literature", the fact remains that Shaktism is still the "prominent denomination" in Bengal in the twentieth century.[86]

We can, therefore, conclude that, despite the increased prudishness of the colonial period, social attitudes towards Tantrism remained largely unchanged in Bengal during the "Hindu Renaissance", because Tantrism continued to remain a strong and vital undercurrent of Bengali culture.

References

1. Bharati (1970 : 267)
2. *Ibid*, p. 270
3. Bharati (1978 : 264)
4. Bharat (1970 : 268)
5. Bharati (1978 : 275)
6. *Ibid*, p. 193

7. *Ibid*
8. *Ibid*, p. 347
9. *Ibid*, p. 191
10. Leonard A. Gordon, in Kopf, p. 89
11. *Ibid*, p. 119
12. *Cf.* William Gunderson, in Dimock (1967)
13. *Ibid*
14. *Ibid*
15. David Kopf, in Kopf, p. 51
16. *Ibid*, p. 52
17. *Ibid*, p. 53
18. *Ibid*, p. 54
19. Suniti Kr. Chatterjee, in Ray, p. 37
20. Ray, Editorial Essay, pp. xxvi-xxvii
21. Dasgupta, p. 76
22. *Ibid*, p. 155
23. William Gunderson, in Dimock (1967), p. 147
24. *Ibid*
25. Clark, in Dimock (1967), p. 89
26. Bhattacharya (1974 : 157)
27. *Ibid*, p. 159
28. Clark, op cit, p. 89
29. Bhattacharya, op cit, p. 156
30. *Ibid*, p. 155
31. Payne, p. 100
32. Van Kooij, Introduction, p. 10
33. *Ibid*, pp. 4-5
34. *Ibid*, p. 5, n. 5
35. *Ibid*, p. 1
36. Van Kooij, Preface, p. vii
37. Van Kooij, Introduction, p. 10
38. Bhattacharya, *op cit*, pp. 134-135
39. *Ibid*, pp. 157-158
40. Bharati, (1978 : 170)
41. Isherwood, p. 89 & pp. 101-102
42. Madhavananda, pp. 195-196 & p. 204
43. Payne, pp. 98-99
44. *Ibid*, p. 4
45. *Ibid*
46. *Ibid*
47. *Ibid*, p. 97
48. *Ibid*, p. 95
49. *Ibid*, p. 99
50. Bhattacharya, *op cit*, p. 161
51. Bhattacharya, *op cit*, pp. 161-163
52. Payne, *op cit*, pp. 102-103
53. *Ibid*, pp. 103-104
54. *Ibid*, p. 104
55. Bhattacharya, *op cit*, pp. 162-163
56. Payne, pp. 104-105

57. Dimock (1966 : 65)
58. Bhattacharya, *op cit,* p. 159
59. Bharati (1961 : 203)
60. Gordon, *op cit,* p. 114
61. Dimock (1966 : 253)
62. Payne, p. 96
63. Mojumder, Foreword by S.N. Ray, p. xiv
64. Bharati (1977 : 112)
65. Dimock (1966 : 249-250)
66. Padoux, p. 276
67. Dimock (1966 : 259)
68. *Ibid,* pp. 43-55
69. *Ibid,* pp. 156-157
70. Bolle, (1962 : 130-132)
71. *Ibid,* pp. 132-133
72. *Ibid,* pp. 137-139
73. *Ibid,* pp. 139-142
74. Bhattacharya (1982), Introduction, p. 26
75. *Ibid*
76. Padoux, p. 273
77. Gupta et al, p. 3
78. Payne, p. 133
79. Gupta et al, p. 3
80. Bhattacharya (1982 : 27)
81. *Ibid*
82. Payne, pp. 2-3
83. Bhattacharya (1982 : 28)
84. Payne, p. 48
85. Gupta et al, p. 28
86. Goudriaan & Gupta, p. 181

7

The Tantric Tradition of Assam: Cultural Implications

ASSAM has been one of the strongholds of the Tantric tradition in India.[1] Since the first flowering of this tradition in the early-medieval period, it has expressed, *and* influenced, the culture of this part of the country.[2] I use the term "culture" in its anthropological sense and therefore, under the "cultural" implications of this cult I shall subsume philosophical, sociological and religious considerations also.

To recapitualate, Tantrism is a distinctive technique of mysticism, by which we mean union with the theologically or otherwise defined ground of being.[3] Tantrism uses the traditional ***mantra*** and ***laya-yoga*** (i.e. ***Kundalini-yoga***) methods, but adds the 'heretical' element of ritualized union with female initiates.[4] The goal is the accepted one of ***moksha,*** i.e. theologically defined emancipation from ***samsara,*** but the means are so antinomian that Tantrism has always attracted the opprobrium of Indian society.

Tantra has flourished in the matrifocal areas of India, viz. Assam, Bengal, Orissa and Kerala. This is not too surprising, because in these matrifocal societies the position of women is better than in the other Indian societies, where the *male* world-view is dominant. These societies are more open, and more amenable to *hedonistic* experiementation than the other, more puritan Indian societies.[5]

At any rate, Shaktism is still a very potent sub-stratum of Assamese culture. Two instances from my own experience as District Magistrate in the Darrang district of Assam will make this clear. First, in the Sipajhar area of that district, the worship of the Goddess Maroi or Manasa is so common that some Muslim people there also take part in the celebrations. I even came to know an old Muslim villager of that locality who could fluently recite from the ballad of Beula and Lakhinder, which is sung during the worship; he told me that he had been visited by the Goddess some years previously, while in a trance-state. Secondly, and more interestingly, one of my senior clerks once told me in quite a matter-of-fact manner that his elder sister, then in her eighties, had in her younger days belonged to the ***raati khowa sampradaya,*** as the Tantric cult is called in Assam.

One of the reasons perhaps why the Tantric tradition thus still survives in Assam is that it came under British hegemony rather late. It, therefore, escaped the deadlier effects of Victorianism. Other Indian societies were not so lucky, and they became puritanical and alienated from the hedonistic-aesthetic heritage of classical India.[6]

Another reason why Assamese society is more open, and hence more hospitable to Tantrism, is that it is also less Sanskritized. Caste is doubtless a powerful factor in social relations, but *not* as much as in the rest of India. Relations between the generations are less strained than in the other, more authoritarian, Indian societies. Male-female interaction is much freer than in other parts of India. All this is incidentally even truer in the case of the *tribal* societies of North-Eastern India, which are perhaps even more open than Assamese society. In such open societies, innovativeness has more positive value than in mainland India, where the regard for the orthodox ***parampara*** stifles individual freedom.[7]

Like all Indian societies, Assamese society also suffers from the male anxiety-syndrome about the loss of the semen virile.[8] This fear is *magical,* because the loss of semen is believed to impede the achievement of ***moksha.*** This is to be viewed in the context of the fact that in India a secular world-view is non-existent, and thus the achievement of the salient religious goals is of paramount importance. Still, this fear is probably less acute in Assam, as in the other matrifocal society of Kerala, in which coitus is not ritually polluting to the Nayars whereas cooked food taken from the wrong hands can be.

Assamese Society Less Inhibited

Since Assamese society is not yet so alienated from its roots in the Indian tradition, religious anxiety, i.e. anxiety about *not* attaining the salient religious goals, is perhaps less prevalent among the incipient middle-class. The people as a whole are thus more cheerful and extroverted than other Indians. This is perhaps also due to the Mongoloid heritage of this society.[9] Thus, this is perhaps one of the very few Indian societies today where there is large-scale singing and dancing, that too for days on end, during the ***Bihu*** spring-festival. During this festival, as during ***Holi*** previously in other parts of India, the entire populace gives itself over to merriment. Other Indian societies are more inhibited, and less able to let go. As of now, when alienation in Assamese society has only just begun, the folk art forms are also still vigorous. Folk drama, music and dance are still enjoyed without the embarrassment with which modern Indians view their traditional culture. All this is in crass contrast to values in the rest of India, where it would seem that to enjoy life is unforgivable !

The modern Indian attitude towards the enjoyment of life is mirrored by modern (urban) Indians' aesthetic attitudes. The sophisticated aesthetics of Mahabalipuram, the Chola bronzes, ***Bharata Natyam*** and the Mughal miniatures have given way to the philistine, Victorian world-view of the British administrators and missionaries. As a result, we have a prominent aesthetic monstrosity like the Birla Temple in New Delhi, which *few* educated Indians see as *appalling* architecture. This is, of course, partly due to the overweening importance of religion in Indian society, where everything has a "other-world" referrent, as a result of which modern aesthetical or other secular criticism has a difficult *entrée.*

In connection with modern Indian aesthetic values, let us also recall Gandhi's attitude towards the magnificent art and architecture of Khajuraho, which he saw as obscene and would have liked to pull down ! [10] Of course, there are silver linings in this black cloud of modern Indian puritanism, like the modern Indian re-discovery of ***Bharata Natyam,*** and Ravi Shankar, and Ali Akbar Khan.[11]

In pleasant contrast to the above polemic, Assamese aesthetic values are reflected in the white ***mekhala-chador*** and red-blouse combination worn by the women, which colour combination is coincidentally the same as that of the ***ida-pingala*** system of ***yogic*** and Tantric symbolism. This brings us back to our starting point. Assamese society today is *still* much less puritanical than other Indian societies. I have tried to adumbrate above the reasons why this is so. The Tantric tradition has been one contributory factor, partly because it has brought in liberal influences (like perhaps ***Vajrayana***) from trans-Indian Mongoloid societies like Nepal,[12] Tibet and Bhutan. On the other hand, the Tantric tradition is itself an expression of the *native* Assamese genius.

References

1. Bharati (1977 : 230)
2. *Cf.* Barua
3. *Cf.* Chh. 4
4. *Cf.* Bharati (1976 a)
5. Bharati (1978 : 336)
6. *Ibid,* p. 340
7. *Ibid,* p. 336
8. Bharati (1977 : 230)
9. *Cf.* Sharma
10. Bharati (1978 : 330)
11. Bharati (1981), n. 3, p. 21
12. *Cf.* Tucci

8

The Kamakhya Myth and Modern Indian Values

As Siva danced in grief carrying Sati's corpse, Vishnu destroyed the body with his discus. Where the pieces supposedly fell, ***Shakta pithas*** were established, throughout the Indian subcontinent. It is interesting that the ***yoni*** or pudendum of Shakti is supposed to have fallen in the North-East, on the Nilachal Hill in Guwahati where the Kamakhya temple now stands.[1] This temple is the most important Tantric shrine in India.

Then there is the legend that the sage Vashistha was sent to the North-East, to obtain enlightenment by learning Tantric ***sadhana.***[2] The temple dedicated to him is situated beyond Beltola in Guwahati. This legend also highlights the hold that the ***Shakti*** cult has exercised in this part of India.

In addition to these, there are archaeological finds like the erotic sculptures in the ruins at Madan Kamdev near Baihata Charali, on the outskirts of Guwahati, which bear witness to the sophisticated aesthetic and moral values of this region of the country. This mature hedonism is a distinct contribution of the Indo-Mongoloids to Indian cultue.[3] The archaeology of North-Eastern India is still in its infancy, but we can use it along with the regional myths to analyse the cultural values of this area, since oral and similar traditions are now being recognized as an important, and in some cases primary, source for the study of cultures. I shall, therefore, use the Kamakhya legend as a starting-point to make a cultural critique of the values of modern India, by juxtaposing these against the pleasure-affirming values of the peoples of North-Eastern India.

Let me begin by referring to a recent controversy in the Indian Parliament, in which objection was raised that Shiva had been called an "erotic ascetic", in a catalogue issued for the Festival of India in the USA. This controversy would perhaps not have arisen if it was kept in mind that, according to the ***shastras,*** Shiva *must* be worshipped in the ***linga*** form; this ithyphallic representation of Shiva denotes the fact that the orgasmic moment is one of the nearest human approaches to the state of desirelessness or ***moksha.***[4]

Dr Suniti Kumar Chatterjee has noted that the Indo-Mongoloids have been quite liberal, in terms of male-female interaction.[5] This is perhaps one reason why Kamakhya is the foremost Tantric centre in India, whereas a Tantric ***chakra*** (i.e. group) in Banaras, in *mainland* India, was broken up by the police a few years back. To take another instance, the Khasis of Meghalaya still have a *matrilineal* social structure.

Further, Audrey Cantlie has recently pointed out that Assamese society is more socially mobile, and has a less rigid caste structure, than other Indian societies.[6] Bharati has commented on the other hand, that in most of India, holding hands and suchlike exhibition of tenderness between men and women are taboo. This is because of the ubiquitous pan-Indian anxiety-syndrome regarding the loss of semen, which loss is believed to cause ritual pollution, and to inhibit the attainment of religious goals.[7] This is very salient in a country like India, which has only very recently imbibed *secular,* i.e. non-religious, values from her British rulers. As part of this syndrome, Indians also equate dark skin with low caste, and find it unaesthetic;[8] at the same time, dark skin is also equated with *uncontrolled* eroticism. In the North-East, which is just getting Sanskritized, these ascetic values have not yet taken firm root. Gradually, however, as the middle classes grow stronger in the North-East, it is likely that these societies will also fall in line with the modern pan-Indian Victorian value systems.

The one great contribution of India to the world has

been the ***yoga*** complex.[9] Modern Indians have, however, become alienated from their cultural roots, and so they cannot appreciate the *genuine* ***yogic*** traditions. They look up to Sai Baba, Mahesh Yogi and similar other bizarre popularizers and self-seekers. In this they follow the trend of the "Hindu Renaissance", from Rammohan Roy to Vivekananda to Gandhi, which we have seen has propagated a hotchpotch brand of Hinduism quite *alienated* from the grass-roots.[10]

Blasphemy Alien to Triditional Indian

In contrast, the North-Eastern societies are still down-to-earth. They are not yet alienated from the sophisticated aesthetics of Khajuraho and Konarak, whose erotic sculptures were dictated by the logic of ***drishti-shuddhi,*** i.e. emptying one's mind of everything, including things erotic, before entering the main sanctum of the temple.[11] It is noteworthy in this regard that the dynasty which built Khajuraho was of tribal origin. The non-alienated Indian sees the numinous in everything, and especially in the most intimate and self-involving situations like coitus. To paraphrase what Gautama Buddha is supposed to have taught: ***samsara*** equals ***nirvana.*** Such a healthy world-view was conducive to humour, whereas modern Indians lack a sense of humour, as the Assamese writer Lakshminath Bezbaruah had also commented. I remember in this context my own experience when I once went around the sanctum of the Padmanabhaswami temple in Trivandrum; on the outside of the sanctum sanctorum, there are a number of carvings depicting scenes from daily life, and I actually noticed one of a person defecating. Thus, the concept of blasphemy is alien to the traditional Indian, more so perhaps to the low-caste artisan who carved the above scene in Trivandrum.

The above syndromes are also significant from the point of view of upcasteing, because as one becomes wealthier one practises more ritual avoidances (which one can now afford to) in order to claim higher status, e.g. by avoiding "boiled" rice and taking only "polished" rice. In contrast, in the North-East, ritualistic avoidance is less rigid; for example, the observation of the monthly "pollution" of women is less eggregious. In some parts of Assam, the onset of a girl's puberty is still celebrated by throwing a feast. And at Kamakhya, the main festival celebrated is the annual menses of the Goddess.

The seasonal festivals are still celebrated vigorously in the North-East: the cyclical concept of time has apparently not yet surrendered here to the Western linear concept. The springtime ***Bihu*** of Assam, and similar festivals of the North-East, are marked by joyous dancing and singing for days on end. Some of these still retain their association with fertility rites. During this spring-festival, elopements take place even now in the rural areas of upper Assam. This sophisticated attitude of personal freedom is a reflection of the *matrifocal* nature of these societies, which are thus more open than other Indian societies. It may be noted here that till recently the system of bride-price was extant in some of these areas of North-Eastern India. On the other hand, in mainstream India we have Gandhi, who had such a profound influence on the minds of young Indians, wanting to pull down the temples at Khajuraho because he felt they were obscene![12] This is in line with his politics of *celibacy*, which he successfully used to become a "saint" in the eyes of the Indian masses. There *are* of course changes taking place due to urbanization, but the Indian women's eroticism is still similarly denied in most parts of the country, except insofar as it relates to her fertility.

Indians have a deep mother-fixation, and the Indian female is glorified as mother, ***sati,*** etc. This is admirable but, as the new discipline of Women's Studies has clearly shown, the effect is to *suppress* woman's erotic and autonomous persona. The *traditional* Indian world-view, however, as illustrated in the myths of mother-son incest to create the world, was no doubt more sophisticated as compared to the sterility and uptightness of the reductionist Oedipal and other Freudian theories. Classical India had accepted all parts of the human experience: everything was sacred, and life itself was ***lila*** or divine play. That is why, perhaps, mental health has not yet been defined as a salient problem in India. This is especially true of the matrifocal and non-aggressive societies of the North-East. It may thus even be claimed that the classical Indian concept of ***Ardhanariswara*** is an apt reflection of the personality-structure in the North-East.

The ascetic and non-hedonistic morality of India is exemplified by the fact that *even* Tantrics view coitus as a *means* to a spiritual end. Their apologetic attitude is shown by their attempts to claim ***Vedic*** status for their minority scriptures.[13] This is responsible for a certain identity-confusion among Tantrics, since they espouse *liberal* values in an overwhelmingly puritanical society. Further, the ***Vedas*** are ***shruti,*** and the Indian veneration of the written word is perhaps responsible for the lack of mature critical attitudes among Indian intellectuals. Of course, another reason for Indians' non-critical and naive attitudes is the Indian veneration of heroes and ***avatars*** like Rama. Indian societies are authoritarian: elders are obeyed, implicitly and explicitly. Gandhi and Buddha are *not* criticized.

Let us now consider Indian aesthetics. In classical Indian drama, there is no concept of tragedy. Classical Indian music is based on harmony, whereas Western music is contrapuntal. Indian poetry is philosophically idealistic : only since Tagore has Indian poetry treated nature as an independent entity. This is perhaps not surprising in a society in which *mystics* are the cynosure: the individual and his works are not important; what is important is the state of mystic union. This syndrome is probably the cause of what others see as Indian fatalism; Indians believe in ***karma,*** and since the Muslim middle-ages, in fate or ***takdeer.*** It is only since the coming of the British that secular, i.e. non-religious, values have begun to take root.

Modern alienated Indians, however, are philistine. Their values are totally ersatz. Indian films are silly and romantic, whereas in actual fact Indian marriages are purely utilitarian, as witness the number of dowry deaths reported in newspapers. Modern Indians are terribly puritanical. They consider it rustic and unsophisticated to take ***thandai*** or ***bhang*** (i.e. cannabis Indica) during ***Holi,*** whereas what they are really afraid of is to let go.[14] On the other hand, ***Holi*** itself has degenerated from the traditional sophisticated merriment into hooliganism.

To sum up, mainland India has *much* to learn from the sophisticated cultures of the North-East. It would seem, however, that the North-Eastern Indian societies themselves are falling prey to the values of mainstream India, as they become more Sanskritized. In fact, part of the etiology of the present political unrest in this region is perhaps this very clash of conflicting values.

References

1. Bharati (1978 : 80-81)
2. Bharati (1976a : 66-69)
3. Cf. Sharma
4. Bharati (1978 : 331)
5. Bharati (1976a), Chh. 8, n. 2
6. Cf. Cantlie
7. Bharati (1977 : 230)
8. Bharati (1978 : 247)
9. *Ibid*, p. 57
10. Cf. Chh. 6
11. Cf. Chh. 2
12. *Ibid*, p. 330
13. *Ibid*, pp. 170-174
14. *Ibid*, pp. 120-121

9

Tantrism and Modern Assamese Ideology

THE term "cultural criticism"[1] refers to a heuristic concept developed by Agehananda Bharati to elicit data regarding the deeply-held attitudes of people as anthropological informants. For example, modern Indians hung-up on Gandhi's "spurious"[2], "Hindu Renaissance"[3] type of spirituality could be one target amenable to the use of this tool; the responses elicited through such inquiry would possibly indicate their underlying fear of loss of the semen virile,[4] and the resultant "archaic" fear of loss of soul.[5] These fears are pandemic to Indian culture, and were thus probably part of the etiology of the Mahatma's politically successful and public celibacy, and resultant sainthood.

My approach here will necessarily be polemical, because that is the very nature of the tool that I propose to use. Also, before I proceed, I should make my own philosophical standpoint clear. Since I will be dealing *inter alia* with aspects of the Tantric tradition in Assam, I should make explicit my mental set, which is that of an admirer of this tradition. I am attracted to this ***parampara*** for aesthetic and moral reasons, and of course according to Bharati the aesthetic and the moral are very likely identical.[6] I shall juxtapose the ***Shakta*** tradition of Assam with the Vaishnavite, and use the above tool (viz. "cultural criticism") as an oblique way of getting to the heart of the modern, official Assamese ideology, i.e. the ideology of the dominant, upper-caste Hindu Assamese groups.

Assam is one of the very few places in India where the Tantric tradition has been, subversively, operational. This is not surprising, because the Assam and Bengal regions have often been called the original home of Tantrism, these practices dating here from the early centuries A.D.

The traditional strength of Shaktism in Assam is due to the large tribal sub-stratum of the society; these tribal groups are till today *even* more matrifocal and liberal as compared to the greater Assamese society, in which itself the position of women is very definitely *much* better than in the rest of India. The robustness of the Tantric tradition in Assam is, therefore, due to the fact that the society and culture have always held comparatively very positive attitudes towards women.

In addition to this great stream of Shakti-worship, there has been another major religious stream in Assam, viz. the Sankardevite brand of neo-Vaishnavism, which has had a profound influence on Assamese culture from the fifteenth century onwards. There are quite a few differences between these two cultural streams. For example, in the Chaitanya-inspired Vaishnavism propagated by Shankardev, we have *group*-oriented activities like ***kirtans*** and ***satsangs,*** where most of the members present are *observers,* rather than direct participants in mystic praxis. Then, the neo-Vaishnavite theology is more authoritarian, and pronouncedly theistic, which means that there is little real philosophy as such in their ideology.[7] Again, like the Sikh ***gurdwaras,*** the Assamese ***namghars*** usually have no idol, only *the* book, viz. the "*Bhagavat Purana*". Contrast this with the healthy polytheism of Shaktism, with its multiple and pulchritudinous female targets for meditation and mystic consummtion.

Further, the neo-Vaishnavite ***sampradaya*** is rather puritanical and anti-woman: Chaitanya inveighed continually against women, and deprecated contact with them. In doing so, however, he was going very much against the grain of Bengali culture, since male-female inter-action has traditionally been healthier and more liberal in the Bengal region as compared to the rest of India; this openness has at least partly been due to the *pervasive* hold of Shaktism and Tantrism in the area. Also, the dour neo-Vaishnavism of Chaitanya was substantially mitigated by the strength of the ***Vaishnava-Sahajiya*** variant of this ***sampradaya,*** as so well-documented by Dimock;[8] this latter erotic Radha-Krishna brand of Vaishnavism did not, however, become so popular in Assam.

Woman an Embodiment of Devi

In Shaktism, as against Vaishnavism, woman is seen as the embodiment of Devi, at least ideally. The tendency in this tradition is monistic, theism being only a stepping-stone to the mystical experience. Further, ***sadhana*** here is individualistic, the goal being to intuit one's union with the divine, the spin-off of its attainment being the experience of personal autonomy in social relationships.[9] Thus, the introduction of the Sankardevite neo-Vaishnavism in Assam, in opposition to the prevailing Shakti-worship, can be considered a dilution of the healthy individualism of Assamese culture, since the former is more group-oriented as compared to Shaktism, as we have seen above. The new ideology can also be assumed to have generated considerable conflict within the culture as regards the status of women; one example is that, quite possibly due to the neo-Vaishnavite brand of Sanskritization, Assamese women (though freer than other Indian women) still have to cover their heads with their saree-ends in the presence of adult males, as is the practice elsewhere in India except for the South.

Also, with the coming of the proselytizing neo-Vaishnavite ideology, the Hinduization of the liberal, tribal sub-cultures became more pronounced, and many tribal people took ***sharan,*** i.e. they became initiated into the Sankardevite cult. These groups became comparatively puritanized as a consequence, and they were absorbed at the *lower*, socially less influential end of the caste hierarchy.

Over the centuries, this neo-Vaishnavite ideology has gradually become the *official* one, and we have seen above that it is comparatively more puritanical than the traditional world-view, especially since the former is held by the *upper*-caste groups. This process is now being accelerated, since the attitudes of these upper-caste elites are increasingly falling in line with those of the pan-Indian official culture, with the improvement in communications with the rest of the country. Thus, these Assamese elites are now gradually coming to share the general values of the pan-Indian elites: they emphasize the less intellectual, less sophisticated and more activist and philistine aspects of the Hindu ***parampara,*** e.g. the *Bhagawad Gita. Ipso facto,* they also venerate Gandhi and Vivekananda, who were the most successful purveyors of the "Hindu Renaissance" brand of the Hindu tradition, spurious though it is in Sapir's terms, as we have already noted in Chapter VI. These tradition-alienated elites are either not aware of, or consciously ignore, the traditional distinction between ***smriti*** and ***shruti:*** the *Gita,* for example, is really only a ***smriti*** and thus has only semi-canonical status, and, therefore, is hardly as authoritative within the tradition as it is deceptively made out to be.[10]

With the greater political domination of the modern Assamese society by the upper-caste elites, and thus with their increasing control of the official machinery, the Sankardevite/neo-Vaishnavite ideology can be expected to become *universal* in Assam, though the Bodo and other tribal groups are already resisting what they call "Assamese chauvinism". The process of *puritanization* of Assamese culture can also be expected to accelerate even *further,* in view of the fact that the pressures of economic modernization are becoming increasingly felt. The patriarchization of Assamese culture will thus become increasingly salient, just as in the case of the matrilineal Nayars of Kerala during this century. There are already disturbing straws in the wind, as when agitating political groups try to ban the usual joyous celebration of the Spring ***Bihu*** festival, in order to further their own factional ends. Of course, the ad nauseam, stereotypical glorification of Sankardev and his neo-Vaishnavite movement has itself considerable *political* overtones; it helps to fill a neo-nationalistic need, since the reformer Sankardev is considered to be the fountain-head of the distinctive, sub-nationalistic Assamese identity.

Before I sum up my argument, it may be interesting here to also have a look at the relative geographical spread of the official ideology. It would seem that in Upper Assam, where there are other powerful lower-caste Hindu groups like the Ahoms, and also substantial tribal populations, the hold of the official, Sankardevite ideology is considerably weaker. Another reason for this could of course also be that Upper Assam is further away from the Bengal region, from where the reformist wind of Chaitanya's neo-Vaishnavism blew into Assam. Thus, the ***Bihu*** spring-festival of communal song-and-dance has basically been a social phenomenon of *Upper* Assam, in parts of which the merry-making at this time of the year goes on for as long as a *whole* month. All this would seem to indicate indirectly that, in terms of female autonomy and so on, the situation is not so bad in Upper Assam, possibly also because Shaktism is still a very strong cultural undercurrent there.

To conclude, I have tried here to use the concept of "cultural criticism" as an anthropological tool, in order to expose the attitudes that lie behind the official ideology of the modern Assamese society and culture. My argument has been that the official Assamese ideology, which is Sankardevite/neo-Vaishnavite, is more puritancial as compared to the traditional ***Shakta*** sub-stratum of the culture, which latter by its *matrifocal* nature is quite liberal in every sense. And this official ideology has of late become even more puritanical, with the accelerating pan-Indian pressures of modernization, and the resultant "technological moralizing" and blandishment.[11]

References

1. Bharati (1978 : 259 ff.)
2. Edward Sapir, quoted in Bharati (1978 : 84)
3. Cf. Bharati (1970)
4. Bharati (1977 : 230)
5. Bharati (1972 : 16)
6. Bharati (1977 : 16)
7. *Ibid*, p. 191
8. Dimock (1966 : 248)
9. Bharati (1977 : 215)
10. Bharati (1978 : 91)
11. Bharati (1977 : 95)

10

Tantrism : A Quest for Personal Autonomy

Tantrism has been suggested as a cure for India's cultural ills.[1] One such ailment is the hypertrophic puritanism of Indian, especially *modern* Indian, society. The erotic sculptures of Khajuraho, etc, have thus, as we have seen in Chapter II, bothered most modern Indians.[2] This is because they have become alienated from the sophisticated concept of ***drishti-shuddhi,*** which underlies these erotic and other depictions of life, and whereby the devotee empties his mind before entering the ***garbha-griha.***[3] Further, the ithyphallic representation of Siva is similarly really an indication of the state of desirelessness achieved in ***yogic samadhi,***[4] and the "divine" is to be seen in every phenomenon, especially in those situations like coitus that affect one most intimately.[5] Thus, one of the most remarkable achievements of classical Indian sculpture is the serenity depicted on religious images, as witness the Buddha images; this is perhaps due to the predominantly numinous, "other-wordly" orientation of Indian culture, which has sought freedom from the human condition in mystical union. Eliade has called this union "enstasy"[6] to denote the joy or ***ananda*** experienced in it. The fascination of Western youth for pseudo-Indian cults like Krishna Consciousness is an indication of this human *need* for ecstasy, however bizarre and spurious these cults may be.[7]

We have already seen that mysticism is the quest for union with the theologically defined ground of being.[8] India has two dozen or so schools of meditation which cater to this quest. Tantra is one such school, which uses the ***laya-***

yoga methods but adds the heretical element of ritualized union with female initiates.[9] The Indian tradition defines life as suffering, and postulates ***yogic samadhi*** as emancipation or redemption. ***Yoga*** does indeed generate an "irreversible poise and inurement to the vicissitudes of life".[10] It generates a satisfying sense of identity, and thus promotes personal autonomy.

The Tantric route to personal autonomy is, however, widely viewed with suspicion. "Fun is out", as Prof. Agehananda Bharati put it, in a personal communication to me in December 1981. A few years ago, in fact, a Tantric ***chakra*** or group was broken up by the police in Banaras. To understand the reasons for this hostility to Tantrism, let us now take a closer look at the pathological puritanism of Indian society.

The English-speaking elite, which articulates the official Indian world-view, has become alienated from the sophisticated aesthetics of classical Indian culture. We have noted that this elite articulates an obsolete Victorian morality, imbibed from the British missionaries and colonial administrators. Indian society is, therefore, highly authoritarian and patriarchal. Women are suppressed, and the Indian male is afraid to show tenderness. This is of course also because of the Indians' magical fear of loss of semen,[11] which loss is believed to impede the quest for ***moksha.*** As a result, Indian society frowns upon the enjoyment of life. The scriptures do speak about autonomy, but this autonomy is only meant for the ***avatar*** or culture-hero like Krishna.

In pleasant *contrast,* the matrifocal societies like Assam, Bengal, Orissa and Kerala are more open. The position of women is much better here than in other Indian societies. It is, therefore, perhaps not surprising that Tantra has flourished in such regions, because such open societies are more amenable to *hedonistic* experimentation.

Mysticism Can be Good Psychotherapy

Western society is also very hostile to such personal experimentation. R. D. Laing and Thomas Szasz[12] have pointed out that Western societies tend to label deviant behaviour as insanity. These writers have shown, on the contrary, that there is really no such thing as "mental illness". Maslow's interest in self-actualization, as also modern radical trends in psychotherapy, indicate that Bharati may be right when he suggests that mysticism can be very good therapy.[13]

In sharp contrast, the "madness" exhibited by mystics has always been given *positive* value in Indian lore. The songs of Ramprasad for instance glorify such "mad" behaviour.[14] They sing of the joy of ***yogic samadhi,*** and Indian sciptures call ***samadhi*** the ***parama-siddhi,***[15] i.e. the highest of the eight or ***ashta-siddhis*** of *yogic* ideology. Even today mystical experience generates personal charisma for the Indian mystic.[16] Modern India is in fact named after the sage Bharata, who wandered about alone, immersed in his repeated ***samadhi***-states.[17] This acceptance of deviant behaviour is also shown by the fact that Tagore used Baul imagery in many of his poems.

Further, the joy of ***samadhi*** is beyond even sensual pleasure, as the ***Brihadaranyaka Upanishad*** pointed out, and thus should be perfectly acceptable to society.[18] The problem, however, is that the mystical experience makes for personal autonomy, and the mystic tends to resent the control of society. Mysticism thus becomes illicit, and more especially antinomian techniques of mysticism like Tantra.

We may also note here that the anthropologist Norbeck has remarked on the role of play in religion, especially in the "rites of reversal" found the world over.[19] And in that context, it is interesting to refer to the traditional Hindu concept of ***lila,*** which views every phenomenon as "divine play", which in other words intuits the numinous in every phenomenon.

In the Indian tradition, the saint who has achieved mystical union is above the norms that rule society.[20] This licence can rightly be interpreted by the mystic as permission to lead his life as he sees fit, without heeding philistine social *caveats*.[21] Such a life is *hedonistic*, bearing in mind that hedonism can be related to any activity, whether Tantric experimentation or devotion to intellectual pleasure. After all, viewed from the perspective of modern ordinary-language philosophy, the "good" man is only a person who is at ease with himself and with society.[22]

In short, mystical union leads to personal autonomy, and Tantra is one such mystical technique. It, therefore, deserves serious, and positive, scholarly attention. It is very much a Great Tradition ***parampara,*** which has survived into modern times, and it could indeed be good psychotherapy for modern India's cultural ills. At the very least, it can be a cure for the boredom that best modern man.[23]

References

1. Bharati (1976a : 299)
2. Bharati (1981 : 17) Cf. also Tucci
3. Cf. Chh. 2
4. *Ibid*, p. 331. *Cf.* also O'Flaherty, n. 52, Chh. I
5. Bharati, *Ibid*
6. Eliade, p. 37 et passim
7. Bharati (1977 : 233)
8. Cf. Chh. 4
9. *Ibid*, pp. 166-168
10. Bharati (1978 : 58)
11. *Ibid*, p. 230
12. Cf. Szasz
13. Bharati (1977 : 194 ff.)
14. *Ibid*, p. 196
15. Bharati (1977), n. 8, Chh. 2
16. *Ibid*, p. 162 et passim
17. *Ibid*, pp. 196
18. *Ibid*, pp. 29-39
19. Cf. Bharati (1976 b), Vol. II
20. Bharati (1977 : 169)
21. *Ibid*, p. 215
22. *Ibid*, p. 98
23. Bharati (1978 : 63 ff)

Bibliography

Aberle, David F. (1966), *The Peyote Religion Among the Navaho*, New York: Wenner—Gren Foundation.

Bharati, A. (1961), *The Ochre Robe*, London: George Allen and Unwin.

_____ (1964), *A Functional Analysis of Indian Thought And Its Social Margins*, Varanasi: Chowkhamba Sanskrit Series Office.

_____ (1970) "The Hindu Renaissance and Its Apologetic Patterns", *'Journal of Asian Studies'*: XXIX. 2,267-87.

_____ (1971), "Hinduism and Modernization", in *'Religion and Change in Modern Asia'*, ed. R. F. Spencer, Minneapolis: Minnesota Press

_____ (1972), *The Asians in East Africa, Jayhind and Uhuru*, Chicago: Nelson-Hall Co.

_____ (1976a), *The Tantric Tradition*, New Delhi: B-I Publications; 1st Indian ed.

_____ (1976b), *The Realm of the Extra-Human*, The Hague: Mouton, 2 Vols.

_____ (1977), *The Light At The Centre, Context and Pretext of Modern Mysticism*, New Delhi: Vikas.

_____ (1978), *Great Tradition and Little Traditions: Indological Investigations in Cultural Anthropology*, Varanasi: Chowkhamba Sanskrit Series Office.

_____ (1981), *Hindu Views and Ways and The Hindu-Muslim Interface: An Anthropological Assessment*, New Delhi: Munshiram Manoharlal Publishers.

_____ (1982), Interview in *Surya:* 26-7.

Bhattacharya, N. N. (1974), *History of the Sakta Religion*, New Delhi: Munshiram Monoharlal Publishers.

_____ (1982), *History of the Tantric Religion: A Historical, Ritualistic and Philosophical Study*, New Delhi: Manohar Publications.

Banton, Michael, ed. (1977), *Anthropological Approaches To The Study Of Religion*, London: Tavistock Publication.

Barua, K.L. (1973), *Studies In the Early History of Assam;* ed. M. Neog.

Bolle, K. W. (1962), "Tantric Elements in Sri Aurobindo", *'Numen'*: IX, 128 ff.

_____ (1965), *The Persistence of Religion—An Essay on Tantrism and Sri Aurobindo's Philosophy*, Leiden: E. J. Brill.

Cantlie, Audrey (1984), *The Assamese : Religion, Caste and Sects in an Indian Village*, London : Curzon Press.

Chandra, Pramod (1955-56), "The Kaula-Kapalika Cults

at Khajuraho", *Lalit Kala:* I-II, 98 ff.

Coomaraswamy, Ananda (1938), 'Tantric Doctrine of Divine Bi-Unity', *Annals of the Bhandarkar Oriental Research Institute* : XIX, 173-82

Das, S. K. (1984), *The Artist in Chains—the Life of Bankimchandra Chatterji*, New Delhi: New Statesman Publishing.

Dasgupta, B. N. (1980), *The Life and Times of Rajah Rammohan Roy*, New Delhi: Ambika Publications.

Derrida, Jacques (1976), *Of Grammatology*, Baltimore: Johns Hopkins Press; trans. Gayatri Chakravorty Spivak.

Desai, Devangana (1975), *Erotic Sculpture of India, A Socio-Cultural Study*, New Delhi: Tata McGraw-Hill Publishing Co.

—— (1981), "Relevance of Tantrism to Erotic Temple Sculpture" in *Madhu: Recent Researches in Indian Archaeology and Art History*, ed. M. S. Nagaraja Rao : 201-215; *M. N. Deshpande Felicitation Vol.*

—— (1984), "Placement and Significance of Erotic Sculptures at Khajuraho", in *Discourses on Siva*, ed. Michael W. Meister, Philadelphia: University of Pennsylvania Press.

Dimock, Edward C. (1966), *The Place of the Hidden Moon—Erotic Mysticism in the Vaisnava-Sahajiya Cult of Bengal*, Chicago: University of Chicago Press.

____ ed. (1967), *Bengal Literature and History*, East Lansing: Michigan State University.

Dumont, Louis (1980), *Homo Hierarchicus: The Caste System and Its Implications*, rev. English trans., New York: Oxford University Press.

Eliade, M. (1958), *Yoga: Freedom and Immortality*, New York: Pantheon Inc.

Forman, Robert C. (1985) "The Hindu Temple—the Metaphysical Architecure of the Kandariya Mahadeva", *Man in India:* LXV. 2, 154-76.

Foucault, Michel (1986), *The History of Sexuality*, London : Allen Lane; Vol, 2, *The Uses of Pleasure.*

Friedan, Betty (1963), *The Feminine Mystique*, London : Victor Gollancz.

Goudriaan, T. and Gupta, S. (1981), *Hindu Tantric and Sakta Literature*. Weisbaden: Otto Harassowitz.

Gupta, S., Hoens, D. J. and Goudriaan, T. (1979), *Hindu Tantrism*, Leiden: E. J. Brill.

Holland, B. (1979), *Popular Hinduism and Hindu Mythology—An Annotated Bibliography*, Westport: Greenwood Press.

Isherwood, Christopher (1965), *Ramakrishna and His Disciples*, New York: Simon and Schuster.

Killingley, D. H. (1977), *Rammohan Roy's Interpretation of the Vedanta*, London: London University, Ph.D Thesis.

Kopf, D., ed. (1969), *Bengal Regional Identity*, East Lansing: Michigan State University.

La Barre, Weston (1976), "Materials for a History of Study of Crisis Cults, A bibliographic essay", *Current Anthropology:* XII, 3-44.

Lannoy, Richard (1976), *The Eye of Love in the Temple Sculpture of India*, New York: Grove Press, Inc.; with Larry Baines.

Lex, Barbara W. (1978), "Neurological Bases of Revitalization Movements", *Zygon:* XIII, 276-312.

Louch, A. R. (1966), *Explanation and Human Action*, Berkeley : University of California Press.

Madhavananda, Swami (1925), *Life of Sri Ramakrishna*, Mayavati: Advaita Ashrama.

Meister, Michael W. (1979), "Juncture and Conjunction—Punning and Temple Architecture", *Artibus Asiae* : XLI.

Mojumder, A. (1967), *The Caryapadas*. Calcutta: Naya Prokash.

Mukherji, Radhakamal (1964), *The Flowering Of Indian Art*, New York: Asia Publishing House.

Nikhilananda, Swami (1974), *The Gospel of Sri Ramakrishna*, New York: Ramakrishna-Vivekananda Center; trans., abridged ed.

Novikova, V. (1976), *Bankimchandra Chattopadhyaya—His Life and Works*, tr. Nishitesh Banerjee, Calcutta: National Publishers.

O'Flaherty, Wendy Doniger (1981), *Siva—The Erotic Ascetic*, Oxford: Oxford University Press; ppb.

Padoux, A. (1987), "Tantrism", entry in *'Encyclopaedia of Religion'*, ed. M. Eliade, New York: Macmillan.

Parkin, David (1978), *The Cultural Definition of Political Response—Lineal Destiny Among the Luo*, London: Academic Press.

Payne, E. (1979). *The Saktas, An Introductory and Comparative Study*, New York: Garland Publishing.

Prakash, Vidya (1967), *Khajuraho*, Bombay: Taraporevala Publications.

Rawson, Philip (1982), *The Art of Tantra*, London: Thames and Hudson.

Ray, Niharranjan, ed.(1974), *Rammohan Roy—A Bi-Centenary Tribute*, New Delhi: National Book Trust.

Ryle, Gilbert (1949), *The Concept of Mind*, New York: Harper and Row.

Saran, Prem (1985), "Tantra: A Hedonistic Quest For Personal Autonomy", *Bulletin of the Assam State Museum*: V, 56-60.

_____ (1986), "The Kamakhya Legend and Modern Indian Values", *Bulletin of the Assam State Museum* : VIII, 114-19.

_____ (1989a), "Are the Sculptures of Khajuraho Obscene?", *Bulletin of the Assam State Museum* : XI, 14-27.

_____ (1989b), "The Tantric Tradition of Assam and its Cultural Implications", in *History and Archaeolgy*, ed. Bhaskar

Chatterjee, Delhi: Ramanand Vidya Bhawan, pp. 84-6; *Prof. H. D. Sankalia Felicitation Vol.*

_____ (1989c), "Attitudes to Tantrism in 'Hindu Renaissance' Bengal, 1857-1947, in *Studies in Indian History and Culture*, eds. R. D. Choudhury and Bhagawan Singh, Delhi: Ramananda Vidya Bhawan, pp. 127-144; *Kanaklal Barua Commemoration Vol.*

_____ (1990), "'Cultural Debate' and, Bengali Attitudes Towards Tantrism", in *Golden Jubilee Souvenir of the Assam State Museum*, eds. Atulananda Goswami and Gunin Bhuyan, Guwahati: Directorate of Museums, Assam, pp. 64-73.

_____ (1991), 'The Hedonistic Element in Religion: The Mystic Chaitanya and His Movement", in *Aspects of History and Culture*, eds. R. D. Choudhury and Bhagawan Singh, Delhi: Ramanand Vidya Bhawan, pp. 97-104; *Ananda Chandra Agarwala Commemoration Vol.*

Sengupta, S.C. (1977), *Bankimchandra Chatterjee*, New Delhi: Sahitya Akademi.

Sharma, T. C. (1983), "The Indo-Mongoloids and Their Contributions to the Culture and Civilization of India", *Bulletin of the Tribal Research Institute of Assam:* I. 1.

Sinha, J. (1966), *Rama Prosada's Devotional Songs—The Cult of Shakti*, Calcutta: Sinha Publishing House.

Sircar, D. C. (1973), *The Sakta Pithas*, Delhi: Motilal Banarsidass.

Szasz, Thomas S. (1974), *The Myth of Mental Illness*, New York: Harper and Row.

Tripathi, L. K. (1959-60), "Erotic Scenes of Khajuraho and Their Probable Explanation", *Bharati* : III.

Tucci, Giuseppe (1969), *Rati-Lila, An Interpretation of the Tantric Imagery of Temples of Nepal*, Geneva: Nagel Publishers.

Van Kooij, K. R. (1972), *Worship of the Goddess According to the Kalikapurana*, Leiden: E. J. Brill; Part I.

Zannas, Eliky (1960), Khajuraho, The Hague : Mouton & Co.

Glossary

Advaita: the most prestigious school of traditional Indian philosophy; its basic doctrine is the essential identity between the "*atman*" and the "*brahman*", which are the impersonal, highly rarefied terms for the individual self and the Absolute.

ananda: bliss, especially that experienced in "*samadhi*", q.v.

Ardhanariswara: the aspect of the great Hindu god Shiva in which he is half-female, that half being his spouse Parvati or Shakti (q.v.).

avatar: a human incarnation of the godhead; e.g. Krishna, who is an "*avatar*" of the great god Vishnu.

Bhairavi: a female Tantric divinity; also, a female Tantric.

bhakti: intense, personalized devotion to a God or goddess.

bhang: cannabis indica.

bhukti: enjoyment; in Tantrism, it refers to sensual enjoyment.

brahmacharya: the stage of studentship in the traditional lifespan; hence, celibacy; it also means mental immersion in the Absolute.

chakra: one of the nodal points (usually six in the Hindu scheme) in the yogic body; see under *kundalini-yoga*.

dakshinachara: the so-called "right-handed" type of trantrism, in which the "*panchamakara*" (q.v.) ritual is performed using only substitutes; a Tantric of this kind is a "*dakshinacharin*".

Devi : Goddess.

dombi : a washerwoman or other person of an untouchable caste.

drishti-shuddhi : one scriptural explanation for the erotic and other sculptures on the walls of Hindu temples, whereby one empties the mind of mundane proccupations by looking at these as one circumambulates the shrine, before entering the inner sanctum.

garbha-griha: the *sanctum sanctorum* of the temple, where the image of the deity is enshrined.

kama : desire, especially sexual.

kama-shastra : works on erotics like Vatsyayana's *Kama Sutra*; these scriptures are semi-canonical in the Hindu tradition.

Kapalika : a member of a Hindu sect of ancient provenance, which practises uncanny acts like living minimally dressed in cemetaries and eating out of human skulls.

karma; lit. action; the traditional theory that one experiences the effects, good and bad, of one's actions.

kundalini-yoga : the esoteric system of yogic meditation in which one visualizes a "subtle" body, which has a central duct called the "*sushumna*" and two helically intersecting ducts called the "*ida*" and the "*pingala*". Along the "*Sushumna*" are nodal points called "*chakras*" where one visualizes various divinities with their respective *mantras* and so on. At the bottom of this yogic body is the Goddess herself, in the form of a coiled serpent ("*kundalini*" = the "coiled one"), which is roused by meditative praxis until she meets her lover Shiva in the crown of the "subtle" body. This union is tantamount to the experience of "*samadhi*", q.v.

laya-yoga : another name for "*kundalini-yoga*", q.v.

lila: the Hindu view that the cosmos is the manifested play of the divine.

linga : sign; also, phallus.

maithuna : sexual intercourse.

mantra : sounds or syllables used in meditation.

marga : (religious) path.

moksha : freedom, religious salvation.

mudra : stylized gesture; an edible used in the "*Panchamakara*" ritual, q.v; the female Tantric partner.

mukti : another term for "*moksha*", q.v.

Namghar : the (Vaishnavite) place of worship of Assamese Hindus.

nirvana : the Buddhist term for "*samadhi*", q.v.

nyasa : the visualization of *mantras*, divinities, etc. at various places of the (yogic) body.

panchamakara : the ritual use of the following five items (or their substitutes), viz. *madya*, akohol, mamsa *(meat)*, matsya (fish), *mudra (an edible), and maithuna* (sexual intercourse)

panchatattva : another name for "*panchamakara*", q.v.

parampara : tradition.

pithas : temples or other sacred places where the goddess is worshipped, often in aniconic form.

prema: a (higher) stage in Vaishnavite *bhakti* or devotion.

sadhana : a programme of more or less intense involvement in religious praxis, usually involving some form of yogic methodology; the male practitioner is called a *sadhaka*, and the female a *sadhika*.

sadhika : see "*sadhana*".

sahaja : natural; it refers here to the doctrine of the Bengali *Sahajiyas*, who believed that sexual love is the natural way to experience *samadhi*, q.v.

samadhi : The Indian term for the mystical experience; it is the last stage in the classical eightfold yoga of Patanjali.

sampradaya : religious sect.

samsara : worldly life with its existential vicissitudes.

Shakta : a worshipper of *Shakti*, q.v.

Shakti : the feminine aspect of the godhead.

sharan : refuge, in god or in some human patron.

shruti : the canonical texts of the Hindus, viz; the *Vedas*, *Upanishads*, etc.

smrti : the semi-canonical texts of the Hindus, viz. the *Bhagavad Gita*, the *Puranas*, etc.

Vajrayana : the Tantric Buddhism of Nepal and Tibet.

vamachara: the so-called 'left-handed' type of Tantrism, in which the *panchamakara* ritual (q.v) is literally performed; a Tantric of this kind is a "*vamacharin*".

yantra : a diagram for meditation.

yoni : the vulva.

Index